ROBBIE WILLIAMS

LET ME ENTERTAIN YOU

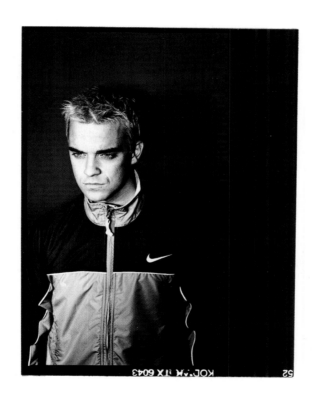

ROBBIE WILLIAMS

LET ME ENTERTAIN YOU

WITH JIM PARTON

Virgin

foreword

I hope you'll have as much fun reading about my life as I have f**king it up!

Take That's whipping boy

Round and about the tents and the mud of Glastonbury there is general agreement that Robbie Williams has been the crowd pleaser of the weekend. 'I didn't expect him to be that good, I just went along out of curiosity,' says one. 'A jolly good time,' says someone else, and from another there is disappointment that Robbie Williams performed in the eight o'clock slot, not last instead of Blur.

But there is another consensus: 'Why does he have to slag off Take That the whole time? Why is he so chippy about Take That? He wouldn't be where he is now without them. They made him. Isn't it time he moved on?'

Well, yes and no.

Obviously, passing the audition into Take That at the age of 15 propelled him into a career as a pop star which he would probably not have had. At that age he had vague ambitions to be an actor, maybe a comic like his dad Peter, or if his mum Jan had had her way, he'd have got A-levels, then gone to university, before thinking about being an actor.

What 15 year old knows what he wants to be when he grows up? For all anyone can guess, if he'd

got that degree, he might have been the North Western sales rep for a central heating company by now. Unlikely, of course, but not as unlikely as becoming a pop star. A part as the Artful Dodger with the Stoke-on-Trent Theatre Company was no preparation for entry into the most successful boy band of all time, but then nothing was.

Actually, it wasn't quite as random as that. His parents separated when he was two, but he hero-worshipped his showman dad ('this bloke who used to come round, take me off to Woolies and buy me a toy car') for starters. His mother, knowing that she had an actor on her hands, encouraged him to take small parts in various productions with the Stoke-on-Trent Theatre Company from the age of six onwards.

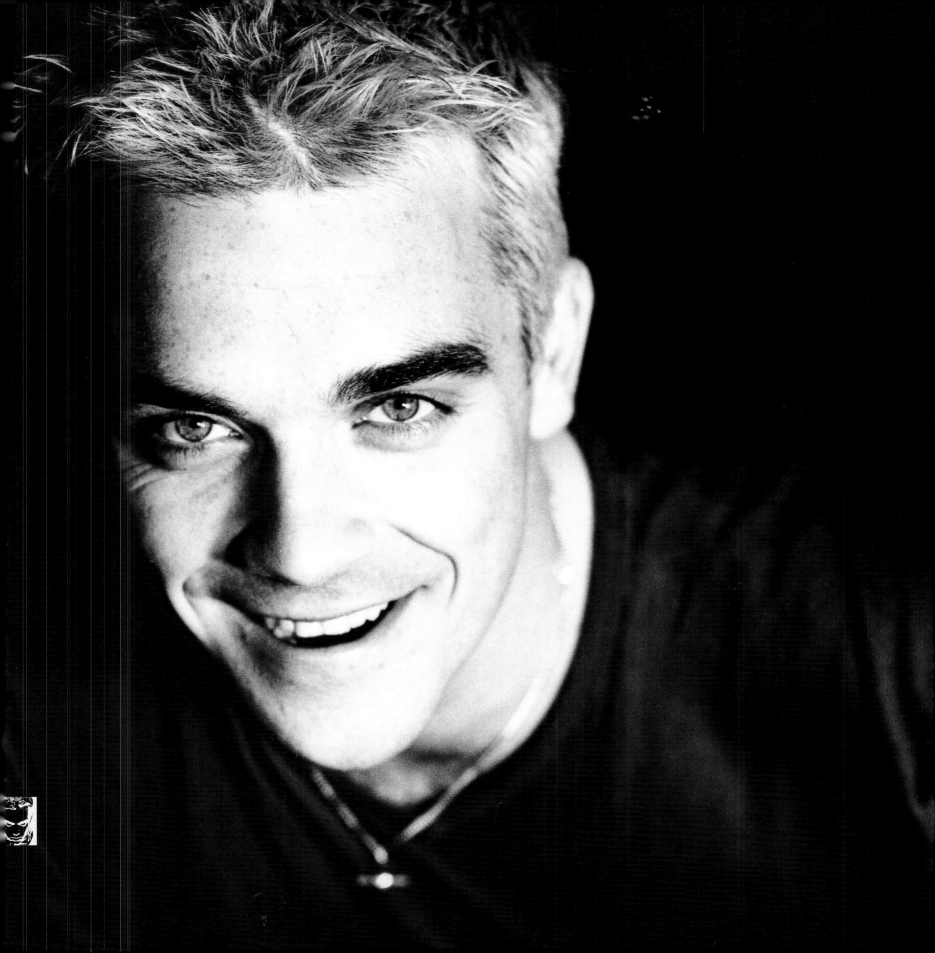

Seven years old.

**The Artful Dodger.
Taken on location in the
Black Country, at 14.**

Having failed all his GCSEs, he frantically auditioned for everything he could, and one of the acts he went for was this group called Take That.

Jan had kept cuttings of local paper reviews, so, when Take That's manager, Nigel Martin-Smith, asked for something to corroborate Robbie's audition performance, she could supply write-ups from the local press that already recognized 'an uncanny stage presence.'

But, yes, without Take That, it is true he'd not be where he is now, and it could be said that it is time to move on from the bitterness of the break. And he is moving on, but the healing isn't complete; so, no, it's not quite time to move on completely.

When his current management, Tim Clark and David Enthoven of IE Music, first took him on, they described a beaten, cowed young man. 'Like a horse that's been abused and doesn't trust the people sent to look after him any more. I'd be chippy for a bloody long

time if I'd felt repressed like that. I mean, if he'd felt able to breathe in Take That it might have been different, but he really did feel suppressed, like leaving an iron bar on top of a champagne cork.'

They took him on in November 1996, when Robbie had had two further bad experiences at the hands of managers and self-styled managers to add to the one under Martin-Smith. The first was with the Mancunian Kevin Kinsella, made bankrupt in 1993, who had been on the peripheries of the music business, and had never managed a major artist. A man who sues when roused (a case against Robbie meanders pointlessly on), so it's probably best not to go on about him too much.

Ditto the next manager, Tim Abbott, who also has a litigious streak and who has also involved m'learned friends in the life of Robbie Williams. Abbott began representing Robbie at about the time Robbie signed as a solo artist to Chrysalis, but had yet to produce any solo recordings. Robbie was in the middle of his one year bender, an addict in severe need of a manager

who was going to sort him out. He got Abbott, a man of great charm, who, record industry sources say, it is impossible to dislike. But the chemistry between him and Robbie was never there. Unfortunately, Tim Abbott was himself a coke user who supplied drugs to Robbie Williams.

Abbott had met Robbie at Glastonbury, just before the break with Take That, when the latter was somewhat under the weather (i.e. pissed and stoned in the company of Oasis, it wasn't muddy that year). It is sad to reflect that when he came out of the band he had already got himself on the slippery slope to addiction.

Back to the beginning though, it is true that Nigel Martin-Smith liked to control almost all aspects of his band's lives. When Robbie passed the audition he was the youngest by about 18 months.

The first couple of years were a struggle, with Martin-Smith finding gigs on the gay club circuit, where the five gyrating adolescents acquired a certain

The Stoke-on-Trent Theatre Company production of *Oliver*.

popularity ('I didn't know that sort of thing happened...' Robbie said later).

There had been a bit of debate in the family about whether Robbie should take the job in the first place. It was a very gay environment. Nigel Martin-Smith is gay. Peter Williams wasn't particularly bothered about Robbie going into that environment; it's the nature of show business to have lots of gay people. What finished the debate off was Rob's Nan who said, 'I'd be more worried if he was going to become a priest.'

There was a time, early on, when Robbie wanted to quit. He quickly began to get frustrated, seeing himself as just another boy dancer. Everyone viewed Gary Barlow as the star of the show, the song writer, musician, the man (or boy) considered to have the talent around whom the band was built. Jason Orange and Howard Donald were amazing dancers, and Mark Owen was exceptionally good looking and could sing a bit. Robbie came into his own during the live shows, where his unpredictable jokiness made him very popular, but he felt himself firmly sat upon if he wanted to express any ideas.

When you consider his current burst of song-writing creativity, it is amazing to think that not one of Take That's songs was written by Robbie; a crime in its way.

As he says, he was happy enough to go along with it for a time, because it was very easy: 'You just turned up and like a robot you just did the thing, but then you began to think you wanted to do something for yourself.'

Being the youngest he felt he became a bit of a whipping boy, the one who was picked on (encouraged by Martin-Smith). His defence was to act up and play the clown; to defuse situations with humour; to become a bit of a cheeky chappie. 'I thought my manager hated me, and that he told the boys he hated me. I thought the boys treated me like an idiot, and that

Robbie at 14.

I was always a scapegoat for everybody else's misfortunes, so it's like, when you feel like an idiot, you act like one, my mechanism against it was to joke.'

When, early on, he announced a desire to quit, Jan and Peter discussed Rob's future on the phone. Peter thought he should stick to it. Robbie told his father he wanted to become a Blue Coat like him, but Peter felt the band had value as a training ground: 'The thing is, there's no apprenticeship nowadays with the passing of the working men's club circuit and cabaret club circuit, so I said to Rob, "Suppose they did have a hit and take off? Can you imagine seeing them on television while you live in a caravan, ironing your own shirts, buying your own toilet rolls?" I think he thought toilet rolls grew in the bathroom. I don't think he'd thought the logistics through.'

So his father and his ever-supportive mum encouraged him to stick it out.

Then Take That discovered girls, or more accurately the girl audience. They were playing at an under-18s club in Hull and the audience went berserk.

And the rest is history, as they say, except that it was quite a hard one when delved into. On the surface there was this spectacular boy band with an amazing live show, up there in world terms in the top 3 with Madonna and Michael Jackson; so successful you could even buy Take That duvet covers (you could choose Robbie or Mark or Jason or Howard or Gary for your pillow case), eight No.1s, 20 million albums sold. A flick of the hotel curtain in Dortmund or Den Haag, and three hundred girls outside would go wild. Robbie would reflect that it was like the *Life of Brian*, 'He's not the Son of God, he's just a very naughty boy...'

They led a life of being smuggled in through the hotel kitchen, and once in their rooms they'd virtually be prisoners, unable to go out for fear of being mobbed. They certainly couldn't eat in the restaurant. As his sister Sally says, 'It was fine for Robert, he had minders, but me, when I was with him a couple of times, there'd be no protection, it was terrifying, one

'There's no career in it, but you

can make a hell of a lot of

money in a short time. But

there's no freedom, every

second of your life is decided

for you, you're a product.'

ROBBIE ON LIFE IN A BOY BAND

time in Berlin I nearly got crushed by screaming girls.'

Backstage there would be a whole amazing infrastructure for absorbing all the girls who'd passed out, with rows of beds, oxygen, and St John's Ambulance ready to resuscitate them. Sometimes they'd have to concentrate on performing at a gig before 40,000 people, while the fans at the front were going quietly purple from being crushed. The astonishing thing is that there has never been any kind of Hillsborough-style disaster at a pop concert.

'It didn't matter that you could sing, because at gigs they were screaming so loud no-one could hear what you sang. I didn't have much of a voice then, I've never had anything like a voice coach. When I listened back to the tape of one of our first singles, I discovered that somebody else was doing my high notes.'

Meanwhile, they were on the most demanding crash schedule imaginable. Robbie would ring his mum and say, 'We're in Belgium,' then she'd hear him being contradicted in the background by Mark Owen saying, 'No, Denmark.'

The schedule was crushing.

Sex, drugs and rock'n'roll.

Sally, the ever-concerned sister, say (talking of the phenomenon of boy bands in general - or girl bands for that matter), 'The thing is, if you're young and want to become famous you'll do anything. You're encouraged to take drugs to keep you going. If you're half pickled it helps you survive, it stops you addressing the real issues. Many agents will have you working seven days a week if they can.'

But then Robbie would say 'Come on, was a teenager. If I hadn't taken drugs and slept with girls when I was in a pop group I would have been abnormal.'

Jan and Sally have always been Rob's big supports, cossetting him when he finally had enough. People would say to Jan about Rob's success, 'Aren't you lucky?' to which she'd ask, 'Why am I lucky?'

The thing about Jan is that she is an intelligent woman and an achiever in her own right, with no need to bask in the reflected glory of her son, which isn't to say she isn't immensely proud. She is, of course.

She has run various businesses, the last of which was a florist and fashion shop in Newcastle-under-Lyme. 'Why' she asks herself now 'did I allow my own progress to stop?' The shop eventually had to close. 'You can't trade with hundreds of Robert's fans about the place. It would have been easier if they were horrible people, but they weren't, they were really nice, the most beautiful young people imaginable, from Germany, Japan, Holland, busloads down from Manchester. I was very fond of them all. Some would write regularly, remember my birthday, that kind of thing, and I've stayed in touch with some. There's one girl from Cologne who used to write or visit every month. She's grown up now. I sent her a wedding card the other day.

'But would I have allowed my daughter to do that? The sheer invasiveness of it.' She spoke out about it to Nigel Martin-Smith, who then came down on Robert. '...but I'm going to speak out about having a hundred fans in my drive bothering me, bothering my neighbours, living with the curtains closed for two years, and I don't care if you are sacked ...'

Finally, the shop had to close. It was things like the arrival of a dying girl in a wheelchair asking for a final wish. Well, Jan would be utterly melted by that sort of thing - she's a giver by nature, nowadays an alcohol and drugs counsellor - and would do everything to get the wish granted. But it was impossible for the ordinary punters from Stoke, who just wanted to buy flowers. As Jan says, 'You can't trade under such circumstances.' So the shop had to close.

Robbie once got a bollocking from Nigel because Peter's mum Nan, always a bit of a character, would sometimes have fans in her house, and this had got written up in the fan club newsletter. But Nan said, 'I will do what I want, he's my grandson and I'm proud of him.'

Jan was a bit of a thorn in Nigel Martin-Smith's side and asked a few too many questions. You could say that she was a nosy parker, but she was just looking after her son and his interests; after all she had to act as signatory on all Robbie's contracts as he was still a minor. She was the one with the business brain, while Robert did not have the time, even if he'd had a business brain (a brain has been discovered since Take That, but business still gets left to other people).

As he says, 'I don't understand figures, and there were a lot of things happening with the accounts and figures with Nigel Martin-Smith and Take That which I didn't understand, so I got my mother to interview the accountant, to find out what was going on. I was travelling around the world and possibly being ripped off for all I knew (or possibly not - I didn't know); I wanted someone to check that, and in my view, if there's not a problem, then my mother should be let in to see for herself.'

Robbie was touring in Australia at the time, and the next thing he knew about the situation was when he was getting in the hotel lift with the boys one morning. The others had been faxed with a copy of a letter from Martin-Smith threatening Jan with legal action. 'Such a vile letter, condemning my mother and making me out as the black sheep of the band... Nigel Martin-Smith was scared of my mother, but he succeeded in turning the band against her.' And against Robbie himself.

Jan is unendingly concerned about her Robert, you could accuse her of worrying too much, but then mums do worry, that's their job. As she says, 'I have always had a total anxiety about his safety. You could say I'm over-anxious, but then I get smacked over the head by something. There is no moment when I am proven wrong about my anxieties. I've had pain in my life, I'd lost my mother when I was nine and a beautiful older sister and a husband I was deeply in love with.'

She describes a kind of telepathy between her and her son; 'Sometimes I've woken up in the middle of the night, it's weird, and I've instinctively known what trouble he was in, having a really bad one.'

And you just have to reflect on the fact that Robbie Williams was a virtual drug addict and alcoholic when he came out of Take That to see that her fears were not exaggerated, and that she was right to voice any she had.

Was Robbie pushed or did he jump of his own accord?

A tour of Britain was planned for the second part of 1995. Shortly before rehearsals were due to start, there was the now legendary Glastonbury incident, when Robbie arrived with a Jaguar bootload of purloined champagne, at or near the Gallaghers' tour bus, got obliterated, and appeared on stage with their band Oasis (a Robbie speciality, crashing other people's gigs). The press had a field day, but insights

into these events are hard to extract from the man himself. The official position on the subject is probably not far removed from reality; Robbie doesn't remember much about it, except that it was bloody good fun.

Being in Take That had felt to Robbie like being institutionalized, like being in a cult. He'd not really been allowed to talk to people, to get different views on things, he'd been cocooned, he couldn't be rebellious or get any knowledge about the world.

'"Why can't I go out there, why can't I do that," I'd ask myself. So one day I went "I've had enough," went and did it. That's when I discovered why I couldn't.'

Certainly, Robbie was as insecure and manipulable as any young artiste. He could never be accused of being thick but he was as green as could be, which amounts to the same thing. One day he'd like to tell the real story, but right now he's subject to a legal gagging order.

Not long afterwards the band and Martin-Smith

were out for a curry one evening. On the surface things were fine, except for the fact that Robbie knew that he was really unhappy.

'I'd realized that I was not the kind of boy to be in a boy band; I have my own ideas and I didn't fit in with what they wanted. I felt I was not allowed to express myself.' As *NME* put it, 'We tried for years to get Take That into these pages. Sadly, a hearty mix of paranoia ensured that all our attempts at altruism were knocked back ...'

That evening, in the curry house, Robbie did not feel that the tensions were unduly strong even when he left earlier than the others. The next day he turned up for rehearsals for the forthcoming UK tour as usual, to be told, 'we think it better if we carry on as a four-piece and do this tour without you. What do you think?'

The gagging order stops him saying what he thought. So, did he resign or was he sacked? Robbie says that, 'this is an issue that is still in my mind.' He doesn't really know. The phrase 'constructive dismissal' springs to mind, but that's one for m'learned friends.

'I've always been straight up about things, and said "I like you, I don't like you, I don't like this," but I didn't feel they treated me the same honest way. That's what I feel bitter about.'

The band was together for six years - longer than many marriages - but Robbie says, 'I don't miss them at all. They were people whom I was in contact with through a certain set of circumstances, and whom, in any other set of circumstances, I wouldn't touch with a barge pole. That happened, you move on.'

It's the same for all of us. It's rare that you choose your work environment, rare that you choose your colleagues.

'It sounds rude, but I don't think they would have chosen me as a friend either.' Although now he is in the lucky position of being able to choose who he works with.

No Regrets
Tell me a story
Where all have changed
And we live our lives together
And not estranged

I didn't lose my mind, it was
Mine to give away
Couldn't stay to watch me cry
You didn't have the time
So I softly slip away...

No regrets, they don't work
No regrets now, they only hurt
Sing me a love song
Drop me a line
Suppose it's just a point of view
But they tell me I'm doing fine

I know from the outside
We looked good for each other
Felt things were going wrong
When you didn't like my mother

I don't want to hate but that's
All you've left me with
A bitter aftertaste and a fantasy of
How we both could live

No regrets, they don't work
No regrets now, they only hurt
I know they're still talking
The demons in your head
If I could just stop hating you
I'd feel sorry for us instead

Remember the photographs (insane)
The ones where we all laugh (so lame)
We were having the time of our lives
Well thank you it was a real blast

Write me a love song
Drop me a line
Suppose it's just a point of view
But they tell me I'm doing fine

The formative years

Once upon a time, Robbie Williams was a megastar. An attempt to slip back into obscurity was an abject failure; he got photographed at all the wrong parties, usually pissed, stoned, or both. 'Blobbie Robbie, Yobbie Robbie.' It's not like America where they worship success, Britain's tabloids like nothing better than having a go at a fallen star.

Now that the star is back in the ascendant, his new fans clamour for important information such as the following: Robert Peter Williams slipped into this world on the 13th February 1974 at the Royal Infirmary, Newcastle-under-Lyme, twin city of Stoke-on-Trent, the much-loved son of Jan and Peter Williams and brother of Jan's ten-year-old daughter Sally.

The family were good Catholics. Jan says that Robbie had an aura about him, even as a child; he was so uplifting to have around. You'd expect an adoring mother to say that about her son, and it's reasonable to discount it accordingly. The thing is that it's probably true, because he still has an aura for the adoring. All those around him recognize that he is a talented, intelligent, charismatic, funny bloke, who

knows exactly where he wants to go and what he wants to achieve, and he is achieving it.

When *Life Thru a Lens* came out, the reaction of the critics was mixed. One asked, '...why, almost uniquely amongst current pop stars, does he attract such sympathetic goodwill from hardened music hacks? ... Perhaps because he just seems like a brilliant bloke, a sparkling personality, so we hope he'll find what it is he's good at and start to get the respect he deserves. Whether it lies in music at all is a moot point, but it sure doesn't lie in the lumpen mediocrity of Britpop...'

Robbie is an entertainer, has been since he was in nappies and used to come down into the lounge of his parents' pub after bedtime (the Red Lion, Burslem, for those pilgrims who need a shrine to

visit). He knew he should be in bed, but he also knew
that if he could carry on getting laughs, he'd buy time
and be allowed to stay up.

Rob's dad Peter is also an entertainer, an old-
fashioned stand-up comedian now in residence at the
Alvaston Hall Hotel, Nantwich. His stage name is Peter
Conway.

As Robbie says, 'I've got a sense of showbiz from
my dad, but it's never going to be the same act. He's an
old-school comedian. Then alternative comedy came
round. Well, I'm alternative pop to traditional pop. It's
the art of self-deprecation. The last thing anyone wants
to see when they're two foot deep in mud at a festival is
someone taking themselves seriously. I can't take myself
seriously because what I do is very silly. It's not brain
surgery that I'm doing, it's not brain surgery that
anyone else is doing, it's just about picking up a guitar
and writing a song and expressing what you want to say
and it doesn't make you Einstein. Like George Harrison
said about the Beatles, "we're just a pop group."'

Peter wonders whether if he'd stuck with his first career (policeman) Robbie would now be whizzing his patrol car up and down the M6 booking people for speeding. As it is, Robbie still hasn't found the time to learn to drive (although he loves go-karting, and his friends say he is infuriatingly good at it, just as he's infuriatingly good at everything).

The family's slide into showbiz started when Peter won £2 in a pub comedy competition (a lot of money, this was a time when a pint cost a shilling - for younger readers, that's 5p), then got into a regional final (£5) and eventually went on to win New Faces the same year that Robbie was born. These days at the hotel in Nantwich he gets asked, 'How come you're called Pete Conway when your son is Robbie Williams?'

Robbie knows what this is like. As a schoolboy he used to get asked, 'If your name is Robert Williams, how come your dad is Pete Conway?'

Peter and Jan split when Robbie was only two, for reasons which are (a) not very exciting and (b) none of your business. At least give a star's parents some privacy.

But in essence, being a restless itinerant comedian who is not greatly interested in pubs was not terribly compatible with being married, so Peter and Jan went their separate ways. He found it hard to regain the heights of New Faces fame - it was a time when the cabaret club and working men's circuit was gradually closing down - and much of his work was far away at holiday camps, like Perrenporth in Cornwall, where he had a four-year summer residency. Robbie would visit, so you could say he grew up with showbiz.

'Dad left when I was two. We've just become mates now, but there's that blood link. My dad is very good at what he does, he's got excellent comic timing, he's so professional, that's what I admire him for. I was too young at the time to remember my parents' divorce. I can't wish for anything more than I've got, with my mum and my sister; what I've got is fantastic.

'I've got a sense of showbiz

from my dad, but it's never

going to be the same act. He's

an old-school comedian. Then

alternative comedy came

around. Well I'm alternative pop

to traditional pop. It's the art of

self-deprecation.'

So I can't say I missed having a father full-time, I mean I don't know, that's the way I grew up.'
The children of divorce may not miss their dads as such, but they often put them on a pedestal in their minds. The unavoidable conclusion is that Peter Williams has been an enormous influence in turning Robbie Williams into the entertainer he is, from comedy through to his love for Sinatra.

Meanwhile Jan, always his emotional support, struggled alone for a while with the Red Lion before selling it and running various other businesses: a dress shop, a café for a period, and at the height of Robbie's Take That fame, the florist and fashion shop that was forced to close.

Not quite alone. There was Sally, who, being ten years older than her brother, was surrogate mum when Jan was busy, and there was Peter's mum, Nan, who remained close to Jan and helped out a lot.

Robbie was susceptible to the paranormal. When he was three or four he'd say things to Nan like,

'There's that lady in the bathroom again'. There was no-one Nan could see. Then he'd say, 'She's gone.'

Peter describes being downstairs in the closed pub one time as he was taking Robert to Nan's. From the corridor there was a window into the bar, which was locked. Robert looked through the glass and said, 'What are those two men doing still in the bar.'

Pete went along with it. 'Just drinking.'

'I don't like them,' said Robert. His expression was startled.

'Well, wave goodbye to them because we're going to Nan's.'

Robert waved at the empty room and the men apparently waved back.

'Dad, they haven't got any hands...'

It made the hairs stand out on the back of his father's neck. But Peter says he is convinced Robert was not play acting.

When Jan describes the aura surrounding Robert she also mentions a spirituality about him and, indeed,

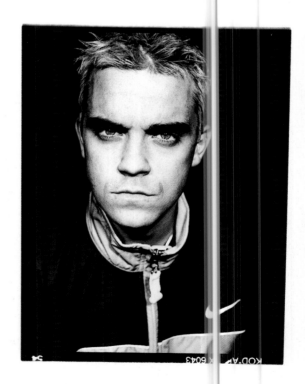

it infuses his lyrics. There's a greater power acknowledged, even if it's not called God.

Angels

I look above
And I know I'll always be blessed with love
And as the feeling grows
She breathes flesh to my bones
And when love is dead
I'm loving angels instead

Some of the music for the new album has been recorded in a studio attached to an old farmhouse near Marlow; there are bedrooms so that there need be no distractions. Robbie had to move into a hotel nearby, complaining that there were too many ghosts and that he couldn't sleep.

When he was eight his mum took him on holiday to Zimbabwe, where they stayed at the Victoria Falls Hotel. There Robert espied Joshua Nkomo, who sat there with two armed guards holding machine guns. 'I said to my mum, "That's the president of Africa." It was the time Lenny Henry was doing his African impressions, and I went up to Joshua Nkomo when my mum was not looking and I said, "Hello, I'm Robert from England and I can do impressions of black men." And then I did my Lenny Henry. He just laughed, then I had a great chat with him. He was fascinated that a kid could just come up to him when he had these men with machine guns, a kid who was not scared. He signed an autograph for me.'

The young Robert Williams (stupid thing to say, he's still young) was good at everything except his school work. He is mildly dyslexic, but that's not the explanation; it's more to do with having a magpie mind flitting around picking everything up but the maths lesson at hand. This is partly what makes him such an alluring performer; you never know quite what he is going to do next. Like getting his kit off on stage in Manchester, 'with only a guitar to cover his modesty.

Nice to know he's found a use for it,' as one paper put it.

It's what a teacher would call a lack of concentration, but it serves him well as a performer; the fact that he has a low attention span and bores easily means that his audience will not be bored. That's the way he is to this day.

The same happens when he's working in the recording studio. He'll do three or four good vocal takes then go, 'I can't be arsed to do this,' and wander out in mid-take.

Nowadays he works with people who understand what makes him tick, but it still rankles that some don't.

Sport is big in Robbie's life, which he gets from both parents. Peter played cricket for Staffordshire and got down to a nine handicap in golf at one stage; while the flame-headed Jan, who Robbie calls 'the freckled flier,' ran for Staffs too.

Robbie was the Burslem Golf Club junior captain at fifteen. He's also a brilliant soccer player. He can do that pro soccer player's trick where they flip the ball over the head and catch it on the back of the neck. He can do this with a tennis ball. So when he scored a penalty for his team Port Vale at a recent pro/celeb match, it was one of the biggest events in his life. Although Robbie is a big Tom Jones fan - 'Delilah' is a Stoke City song - Stoke's opposition know that, to wind Stoke up, all they have to do is play 'Angels' over the tannoy at half time. Last season both of the Potteries sides faced relegation struggles, but Port Vale stayed up and Stoke went down. Ha!

His bedroom had pictures from *Shoot* and *Match* on the wall. 'The whole Oxford United team had one bollock hanging out, that was my favourite.'

In later times, a newspaper was commenting on his rivalry over debut singles with Gary Barlow: 'The rivalry to make it big in their solo careers intensified after Robbie branded his old mate's song as "awful" and said next time he wanted to meet Martin-Smith

Hello Sir

Hello Sir, remember me?
I'm the man you thought I'd never be
The boy who you reduced to tears
Lad called 'thingy' for six whole years.

Yes, that's right, my name's Bob
The one who landed the pop star's job
The one you told, look don't touch
The kid who doesn't amount to much.

Well, I'm here and you're still there
With a fake sports car and receding hair.
Dodgy Farah trousers that think you are smart
Married to the woman that teaches art.

Married to the life, married to the school
I wanna sing and dance Sir; now who's the fool?
Sing and dance, you thought I was barmy
Settle down 'thingy', join the army.

And who are you to tell me this?
The dream I want I'll have to miss
Sir is God, he's been given the right
To structure lives overnight.

Now I know life's true path
Tanks and guns that'll be a laugh
No, not me I'm a mega civilian
I won't lead my life riding pillion.

But thanks for the advice and I'm sure it'll do
For negative dickheads just like you.
As for now I've a different weapon
Stage and screen is about to beckon.

And here I sit in first class, bollocks Sir, kiss my arse ...

was "at the wheel of a fork-lift truck going 100mph." He later apologized for the outburst, blaming England's Euro 96 defeat by Germany for his bad mood.'

Somehow it is to be doubted that his heart was in the apology, that the normally honest and open Robbie Williams wasn't being a touch disingenuous. There can be little doubt that if he were to meet Martin-Smith again (which he hopes not to), to be at the wheel of a fork-lift truck going 100mph would be ideal.

An early predilection for the bottle surfaced at age thirteen, when he got drunk while his dad was doing comedy at Scarborough. The barman kept slipping him Newcastle Brown. He got drunk for the second time at fourteen, at home with a friend, waking up to disarray and to find the glass of his signed Muhammed Ali picture smashed. He couldn't remember a thing about it.

And one reason given for failing his GCSEs was that he took them on acid. But he became a heavy drinker in his late teens in Take That, giving his surrogate mum Sally a lot of anxiety because there was

not much she or Jan could do to help at that time.

Peter sings as well as makes you laugh, 'in a Sinatra style,' he says. His heroes include Sinatra, Ella, Nat King Cole, and he thinks these days Barbra Streisand has the best larynx around. Jan has similar musical tastes. Sinatra and Robbie Williams might seem about as far apart as you could get, but you'd be wrong if you thought so. Frank is a big hero of Robbie's, being (like Tom Jones) the combination of consummate singer and actor-showman - and he's absorbed every one of his tricks. Robbie's Sinatra impression is right up there with his now famous Tom Jones one from the Brit Awards. Brilliant.

But he's not good at everything. Just before Take That Robbie spent a brief period as a double glazing salesman. Not that he ever sold any double glazing. One of Sally's boyfriends got him the job, one to which any 15-year-old boy was ruinously unsuited, but particularly Rob. He rang up his dad and told him, 'I'm being told to eff off all over Staffordshire.'

Rescued from oblivion

'Rob was upset when Take That finished. They were so overworked I don't think he was particularly well. He was extremely run down. I sometimes think that had Nigel Martin-Smith said they could all have four months off it might have lasted longer. They all badly needed a break.' So says Peter Williams.

It would be almost exactly two years from leaving (or being fired from) Take That in July 1995 before he came out of rehab clean, ready and able to pursue the career that a man of his talent deserved.

And what happened in between? A lot of it has been covered in the press, some of it true, some of it not. *NME*'s 'Ligger of the year 1996' was one award well earned, but to come in at No.26 as 'Most Shaggable Man' behind Richard Gere in one survey was something of a setback, even if another had him at No.2 as 'Most Kissable' behind Prince William, who at the time had the unfair advantage of beauty by association with his absurdly famous and photogenic mum.

Professionally, there is a one-year black hole in Robbie Williams' life which is difficult to account for, beyond saying that it took until June 1996 for Robbie to escape from RCA, Take That's label, to EMI's Chrysalis. Shortly afterwards came the release of the George Michael cover 'Freedom' at the end of July. Quite what went on in between is difficult to quantify, even with the help of Robbie Williams. It is clear that the boy showed some form, but equally clear that he is unwilling (or just as likely, unable) to catalogue what. It's all vodka under the bridge.

It is well documented that he went to a showbiz party on New Year's Eve 1995 and moved in with a girl he met there on New Year's Day (Jacquie Hamilton-Smith). Over the next year Jan and Sally would get the odd message from him like, 'Mum, I'm in Cornwall,' or, 'I'm OK, I'm in a pub,' as if that would reassure them, until he brought his bag back to Jan's on New Year's Day 1997.

'That was some party, mum.'

The press were rapidly writing him off as the next Andrew Ridgeley to Gary Barlow's George Michael. Pop star years should be measured like dog years, they were saying (there's nothing wrong with cliches, they so often become cliches because they are both true and a neat way of saying things). The press delighted in writing up the state of the betting amongst 'record industry insiders' as to when Robbie would die of an overdose. Hilarious stuff. If he really had died of an overdose that would have sold a few newspapers, which was all he seemed good for at the time. Selling records? Forget it.

There were acres of print on Blobbie Robbie and pies and his new corpulent appearance, or Yobbie Robbie the Liam Gallagher clone.

Gig crashing is a bit of a speciality. 'It was spur of the moment. I was with Oasis doing *Top Of The Pops*. They were doing *Top of The Pops*, I was just hanging out and I was completely off my trolley. I just decided to take myself off for a walk and ended up on the *EastEnders* set where I said, "Can I be an extra."' So he has a Hitchcock-style

vanishingly quick cameo appearance on *EastEnders* to his credit, sitting in the bar taking a phone call.

One tabloid article pictured the new, fat, pie-eating Robbie, next to 'today's menu' (steak and kidney pie lunch, takeaway pizza dinner, etc.) against a svelte, slimline, boyish picture from Take That days. The trouble is that the old picture had had the waist shaded out to make him look even more svelte than he ever really was. The dishonest bastards. Don't you just hate the press?

He has a scary story from that period too, reminiscent of ghostly occurrences in the Red Lion in Burslem. 'I'd moved into a house with a girlfriend of mine, when things started to happen. The music would come on upstairs for no reason. Then there were windows shutting and closing, doing daft things, and then the Banham locks started shutting, closing. The Banham locks...' Robbie pauses so that you get the sheer impossibility of Banham locks moving on their own.

'Then tables would move in front of me. Furniture would move around. People would run up and down stairs and it got to the point at night where they were running around the bottom of my bed. Now, these may be delusions, drug-induced psychosis, or whatever, because I was pissed a lot at the time, but anyway, the girlfriend would say, "don't be silly, go to sleep", but I couldn't, so I'd take a bottle of vodka to bed with me to get to sleep, and sleeping tablets. Then I'd wander around the house naked with a bottle of vodka, going, "come on yer buggers yer don't scare me," because nothing scares you when you're pissed. It got to the point when they were running around my bed one night and I said, "I'm going, I'm off."

'I thought they were in the air each time I went down to the pub. Anyway, I went and left and stayed at the Swiss Cottage Marriott Hotel.

'I was telling the story to a new friend, a good friend now. "If it had stayed with me, I would have had to kill myself, it was that bad," and the friend just looked at me blankly. I thought, "He thinks I'm mad. Go on, say something." But he just looked at me, then he said, "I didn't suffer it for three weeks, I suffered it for seven years and

it put me in a coma. What did you say you did? Me too. I moved out and I went to the Swiss Cottage Marriott Hotel.'" Creepy.

It emerged that Robbie's friend had been staying in the same road. It was some land the Duke of Westminster had bought off the church. 'It turned out to have a Black Death burial site underneath it.'

We digress. Back to the press; Chrysalis Records were reported to have put Robbie Williams in a health farm, where, apparently, 'he's eating fewer pies'. Absolute nonsense; record companies don't put their signings in health farms. The management should encourage, even cajole their artist into sorting himself out, but at this time Robbie was not supported by anyone with thoughts of health farms. Abbott once rang Robbie up when he was in Miami, trying to get songs written with Desmond Childs.

'You're buzzing, I'm buzzing, we're going to storm the world.' What could he have meant? Prat.

Robbie's lucky break was being signed by JF Cecillon

at Chrysalis Records, who arranged the songwriting experiment with Desmond Childs and Eric Bazilian. But getting signed by Chrysalis was by no means Abbott's achievement; Virgin and London were also interested, in fact, virtually any label would have signed Robbie, given that he was a big star coming out of such a big band. Even so, it's difficult to understate how lucky this was (beyond commenting that you make your own luck, and Robbie is talented) when JF, as he's called, put his 'big French bollocks' on the line.

Remember the big boy bands of yesteryear? The Bay City Rollers? Can you name them? How many of them have made it as solo artists? Or the Osmonds, other than Donny and Jimmy? Or the Monkees? When JF signed Robbie Williams in July 1996, it could have been like signing the Bay City Roller, Les McKeown.

However, as a financial investment, Robbie Williams was not all downside. Remember, the Bay City Rollers still tour Japan.

But, on the face of it, JF was signing a dopehead,

pisshead performer who could gyrate pleasingly for a crowd of teenage girls (who would soon grow up), but who had never written a song, and had no obvious talent beyond being a performer who'd survived for six years in the biggest boy band of all time - not a feat to be underestimated. There was no hint that he could write songs, that he had ideas of his own.

Signing him was a gamble. So why sign this bloke who'd left Take That under a well publicized cloud? (not of hashish, it was far worse).

JF had gut instinct. Gut instinct is crucial in the music business, in any art, (imagine if you'd signed Van Gogh, who didn't sell a picture in his lifetime).

But these days the industry is much more grown-up than it used to be; the main companies are so far from the 1960s underground they're even listed on the Stock Exchange, for God's sake. Indeed, the industry is now so professional, so imbued with the business school ethic, that 'gut instinct' is something you simply don't mention; not unless you want your career to last in dog years, or pop

star years, which of course record company executives don't. They like the security, and the pension plan, and a retirement to a country house and horses, even if a bit down the scale from Paul McCartney's.

JF didn't know whether or not Robbie had any ideas of his own, and in the sozzled state in which he was signed, the job interview would have revealed precious little either. It's vulgar to talk about money, but after Robbie's contractural problems had been sorted out and a new deal signed he had enough net worth to be an excellent marriage prospect.

They paid him a lot, so JF's instincts had guts. Or balls. Big French balls.

JF Cecillon was very into people he thought of as 'stars', and he saw Robbie Williams as an authentic pop star. According to conventional wisdom the more obvious person to sign from Take That might have been Gary Barlow, the lead singer, songwriter, the man around whom the band had been built. Watching the videos again five years on, they don't give much of a sense of why Robbie

would be worth signing. He seems to be just a boy dancer, there to provide some sex appeal.

Maybe Gary himself is the best person to explain. 'I was the only singer to begin with ... then all of a sudden Robbie developed this voice and when Robbie sang he really sang, it gave me goose pimples. He's a great singer when he puts his mind to it, he gets it spot on. That was a bit of a worry for me because I knew he could be the best singer in the band. But he never worked at it, so he never was.'

'I'm just a musician, I'm not a performer like Robbie who can blow a crowd away.'

'I really want to see him make a hit record, to give me goose pimples like he used to. Robbie's the best performer in Take That, honest to God. If people were to see him on stage he'd blow them away. It's not too late for him. If Robbie waited two years it wouldn't be too late, because he's just so good that no matter what he's done, his talent will outshine all of it.'

So there you have it.

Chris Briggs was the A&R man assigned to JF's 'big French balls' mistake. As he says, 'There was no particular buzz around Take That about Rob. A small number of people outside understood he was special; amongst the fans, he would have been many people's favourite That along with Mark Owen.'

Robbie would describe his broader appeal as follows: 'I was the lads' favourite. Closet Take That bloke fans liked me. I'd be second behind Mark in the most desirable stakes among the girls ... but I won best haircut a few times.'

He's being a touch disingenuous, understating his own abilities, in which, quietly, he firmly believes. He makes light of it but he is ambitious, driven, and urgently wants to succeed. Sozzled he might have been, but he still had ideas and knew that ultimately he was the only one who could dig himself out of the hole he was in.

Briggsy, as he's known (which makes him sound like the rear gunner in a Lancaster), explains it thus: 'You know there are doctors in Harley Street who are called third or fourth referral doctors, who handle patients with

curious symptoms who've had a battery of tests, and tried various treatments which are going nowhere. There's the doctor who is a specialist on picking up on cancer early, when other doctors just don't get it. There re vets who can do it with horses.' Briggsy spends his quality leisure time knee-deep in horse shit in his country ouse. He was one of very few to take a pastoral interest i Robbie, to sympathize with his addictions and spot the resplendent butterfly trying to escape from its, er, chry alis.

So, having been signed by JF, Rob's ne stroke of luck was to be referred to Briggsy.

(An 'A&R' man? One of those terms spl ttered about the music press, and if you challenge, no-on knows what it stands for. 'Artist and Repertoire'. 'Look, ve got this singer called Frank Sinatra, find him an orc estra, find him a song.' The traditional A&R man's job w s to think, 'Nelson Riddle would be good for Frank, and ll get Irving Berlin's mates to write some songs.')

'Unfortunately, The Beatles made it co pulsory to write your own songs to be taken seriously. But until it

was realized that inside Robbie there was a creative artist trying to escape (not just a performer) it seemed that an old-fashioned A&R job needed to be done.

Chris Briggs met Robbie for the first time when he was starting to record the George Michael cover 'Freedom'.

'Robbie didn't look very comfortable at all. 'Freedom' had been JF's idea. JF wanted something out ASAP, because there had been such a long gap, any single would do. It didn't have to be a classic work of art, it was a pragmatic decision to get something out because young pop stars evaporate very quickly. The sentiment of 'Freedom' fitted Rob's situation. He kind of did it under sufferance, although I don't think it's anything like as awful as he thinks.'

The record company was still trying to promote a Boy pop star, while Robbie, all the time fighting his demons, his addiction, the feeling of rejection from Take That, was trying to come up with ideas to move himself off in another direction, as yet undefined.

The process was slow, but Chris Briggs was the first at Chrysalis to begin to latch onto the fact that Robbie needed to explain to somebody what it was he wanted to do, had his own ideas but didn't yet feel comfortable expressing them.

Briggsy remained hazy as to what these ideas were, or as he puts it rather more grandiloquently 'I try not to over-analyze these situations. If you do, sometimes you smother them.' (Code for, 'I hadn't a clue what was going on inside the head of this young artist.')

He also had the instinct, born of years of experience of dealing with brittle artists proving too brittle to maintain a certain distance. He describes the process of 'More like gardening than anything else. You have to be very, very patient.'

The horse shit he shovels at weekends (one assumes) goes on his roses (which, one also assumes, bloom profusely), unless he's bullshitting (but he's not - *Life Thru a Lens* could even become 1998's best-selling album).

Early attempts to apply manure to the Robbie Williams

bush (or even prune it) were not notably successful. They knew he could perform but it was to be some time before Chrysalis discovered his broader abilities. He could also write lyrics, and the big unexpected thing was that ' ... he's also got, and I don't even know if Rob appreciates the degree to which he's got it, melody ideas which are very good. He'll sing something to you, Lionel Bart had an old girl who played piano: it's the classic 'I'll hum it, you play it' thing.'

Robbie had somehow got it into his head that if you aren't a maestro guitarist you can't be taken seriously. But as Briggs says, 'That is nonsense. The important thing is the ideas, not the technicians. (Most guitarists would not consider themselves as technicians, but we get his drift.)

'I was presented with finding what was there, if anything. Rob had good ideas of his own. He read me some of his lyrics, which were very good, and the fact that he had "Old Before I Die" in his head showed he'd have something to contribute to songwriting as well as performing.'

'In my job I could be forced to use my technical skills to work with any artist. "Look Briggsy, we pay you all this

money"' - which I spend on horses, he might have added. It would be some time before the rose began to bloom, and several more gardeners would become involved with the pruning and application of manure.

Enough of that. Robbie Williams is not plant life.

One idea that JF had, which didn't work but which Briggsy had to carry through, was for Robbie to go off to Miami and work with Desmond Childs and Eric Bazilian (the team behind many Jon Bon Jovi songs).

'In anything creative it's trial and error. People who don't work in the creative end think that it's all a whole lot more planned out than it is. But really it's informed experiment - experimenting, but with a lot of experience. The theory being that you know that a lot of things won't work out, but you try to narrow your experiments down so that you work in a reasonably narrow band where things have got a good shot at succeeding.

'I've sort of absorbed thousands of songwriters' styles and if somebody says to me, "Who should write for so-and-so?" I have a think for half an hour and then I get a

read-out of five or six names. I know Desmond. I know Rob. I would never have thought of putting those two people in the same room. Some artists I work with are perfect for Desmond, but Rob? Never.

'When we got to Miami, Desmond had already prepared three song ideas before we came. Well, lyrically, the moment Desmond started talking, I mean Rob's face, you should have seen it ...'

Or, as Robbie puts it: 'Desmond does what Desmond does. A guaranteed hit, and they are guaranteed hits with Desmond Childs. Guaranteed. Desmond is a nice man, a lovely man, but I was raised in Stoke-on-Trent, and I went to the pub, and I have a different outlook on life from someone who's lived in Miami all his life, writing songs for Jon Bon Jovi. I don't want to slag him off. He does a job for certain people, but it's not for me.'

If he were a little more pretentious he might say, 'Adult American pop, listen, this song just has not got that British, post-modern ironic feel to it ...'

But the real reason Robbie agreed to go to Miami,

against his own instincts, was that Tim Abbott, at every turn, was pressurizing him to do what the record company said. Robbie felt that Abbott was unhelpful when it came to developing his own ideas.

Robbie had the kernel of 'Old Before I Die' that he'd been singing in the back of the taxi on the way to Heathrow, which was encouraging, but it was obvious to Briggs that Robbie didn't feel entirely comfortable about the trip, even before the two had left the seafood bar at terminal four to board their flight.

'Childs was professional to a fault. You'd have had to be the most insensitive person alive not to realize that Rob was doing his best, but that his heart just was not in it.'

Robbie was also doing this because he liked JF Cecillion. He had to make a go of it, and from Briggsy's point of view it was a way of going through the motions, if only to convince JF to agree to try out whatever the next thing was going to be.

They were all for taking an early flight back, but JF threatened to fly out, so they had to stick it. 'Rob and I had got into this routine in Miami of going out for sushi, and I'd look at Rob, and he didn't even have to say anything. I'd go, "I know, I know; only, look, just two more days, alright, and we'll be back in London."'

But it wasn't a completely wasted trip. They got to know each other, to build an understanding of the kind necessary to help Robbie rebuild a career once Robbie had either had the 'technicians' found for him, or had come across them for himself.

'Even if he hasn't got any songs written, I work on the basis that the artist knows best; I'd got to that stage with Robbie, and he was starting to brief me almost, giving me actual names of people he liked.' Robbie's self-confidence was so low that although he'd plenty of ideas of who he might like to work with, the kind of people he'd really like to work with were way beyond him (Frank Sinatra).

And from an outsider's point of view he was still looking like the next Andrew Ridgeley, worse, one who ate a lot of pies (the perfidious press, slow off the mark, never picked up on his new love for sushi).

It all began to fall into place when Robbie hitched up with his current management team of Tim Clark and David Enthoven of IE Music.

Crunch time came with Tim Abbott (he's been crunching ever since). Abbott rang Jan for the nth time to protest about Robert.

'Why do you bother with him?' she asked not unreasonably. 'It's not working out, why not call it quits? I don't want any more phone calls. I'm not his manager, I'm his mum.'

She told Robbie he needed to go shopping for new management, to get a list drawn up by his accountant Richard Harvey, someone they trusted and who knew a lot of people in the music business. Robbie interviewed half a dozen different managers and reported back that he'd felt immediately comfortable with David Enthoven and Tim Clark. He'd been up front about all his problems and they'd understood. Jan told him not to get too excited but to leave it a few days, then talk to them again.

Tim and David would cheerfully (they've lots to be

cheerful about these days) characterize themselves as a couple of old dogs well past their sell-by date (in record industry terms). They're in their fifties, as is Briggsy, with whom they go back a long way.

This allows them to go on at great length about everything, sorry, call on their depth and breadth of experience.

Tim started by selling 'ska' to the Jamaican community and mods, and David as a roadie, long ago. 'We still have a certain idealistic fervour about music and art, it's business of course, but we do like to think we're working with people with real talent. We're frustrated artists ourselves, to a degree, both came into the business at a time when it was the underground and we were fighting big corporations, now we're doing the same, but on the artist's behalf, not our own... Most of the industry these days is run by executive types out of law schools or advertising agencies, two places I'd never want to go,' says David.

David was managing King Crimson and signed the band to Island Records where he met Tim. David had started his phenomenally successful management company and record label EG, working closely with Island Records, the most successful and hippest record company founded by the legendary Chris Blackwell. David managed Bryan Ferry and Roxy Music who Tim had signed to Island Records. This working relationship flourished until the EG roster left Island. The two drifted apart but never lost touch. In 1991 they decided to work together again on a number of different projects, and they were commissioned by Virgin to sort out Massive Attack for an 18-month period, acting as advisors to the band's bright but then inexperienced manager. A nice little shop window, along to which Robbie Williams came shopping.

They didn't know much about Robbie - beyond that he was a star out of a huge band.

They were just interested in meeting him. They found a young man not in the best of shape, very unhappy, not a little bitter, mixed-up and angry. What he needed was a strong team to support him. He felt that all the bad jokes about what a manager could do to an artist he'd had done to him. Robbie played Tim and David some of his demos, which were OK as music. But then he started spouting poetry to them. They looked at each other in surprise and amazement, and didn't need to say, 'All we've got to do is find a musician to do that with him.'

Between their first meeting and becoming his managers they were in a several-thousand-strong audience of music industry professionals when they saw him compere the MTV music awards. All sorts of things went wrong, with technical failures, loss of microphones, and Robbie left high and dry with a highly demanding audience as the broadcast was interrupted for advert breaks and the like. Through it all shone Robbie the performer, who managed to keep the show going despite near-chaos reigning all around – and despite being at, probably, his lowest ebb.

They'd gone into the first meeting with Robbie out of curiosity as much as anything, with no idea what they were going to find, if anything.

But they'd seen him save what could have been a fiasco through sharp wits and coolness under pressure; in short, sheer professionalism. Indeed Robbie had prepared himself for this with no managerial help - he even went on the wagon for a week beforehand.

Then there were the lyrics. 'There was absolutely no doubt in our minds. This was a guy who was writing poetry from the heart, really genuine, tearjerking stuff, very sincere. He also had unexpectedly strong musical ideas.'

So their first task was to find a suitable musician to help get Robbie's ideas sorted out, and the other still elusive 'technicians'. Even so, agreeing to manage him was not that obvious a decision; Robbie was in a mess, a liability. But he walked into a lucky office. 'A couple of old dogs, who'd been there and done that, we knew exactly what was going on. David more than I,' says Tim.

'I love that,' says David. 'Tim escaped by the skin of his effing teeth. But yes, back in my past - ' and remember, in an industry that embraces youth, these men are very old, 'been there, done that' was an expression invented for

them ' - I went off the deep end and drowned basically. Tim and I, we've seen people die, some of our great mates.' They reel off a list of their great mates, the famous departed of yesteryear.

But with Robbie they began to realize that they had 'a really special young man' on their hands, and by talking to him over a period of time they gradually uncovered someone who was highly intelligent, very bright, and knew exactly what he wanted to do and achieve, but without a clear idea of how to do it. So, as with the horse that has been beaten, they set about slowly building up trust with him.

The first thing was to help him decide on an 18-month game plan, including the release of an album and the start of building a new audience. They'd also won the trust of Jan, who was very, very supportive of what they were doing, after Robbie had gone home for a bit, having not been well. They went up to Stoke, sat down with her, and during the course of a really good chat found that they were coming from the same place as she was, and that they

could combine with her and Sally and become a unified team. Nowadays, Jan calls them the 'two proud dads'.

They spent until November 1997 setting out their stall; their strategy not as obvious to the gainsayers as one might think. They were told on many occasions, including by many at Chrysalis, 'You're mad, you're throwing away all your audience,' when actually what they were doing was trying to get a new one, because the old one (screaming teenage girls) was shrinking anyway.

The enterprise was a gamble at this stage, because although they were certain of Robbie Williams as star material, they had a lot of people to convince, plus there remained outstanding litigation from Abbott and Kinsella; but the gamble has proved a good one. They've set about building a hand-picked team of tour and production manager, sound engineer and lighting designer, and they've had 'a hell of a good time doing it.'

The final lucky break Robbie needed was to find the equivalent of Lionel Bart's old girl on the piano to hum his tunes to. The Desmond Childs, Eric Bazilian combo hadn't worked, and there was no-one in particular on the horizon.

It came when they found Guy Chambers. (Guy must have been wondering when he was going to finally appear in this book, because, in the ensemble, he is very important indeed.)

Paul Curran of BMG Publishing had sent a tape of Guy's stuff speculatively to Tim and David. Paul had signed Horace Andy, another IE Music client, so they'd worked with Paul before. Paul Curran is another 'not-so-old-dog' of the music industry.

Meanwhile, Briggsy had been trying various other things in the desperate search for somebody compatible with the talented but mercurial Robbie Williams. Robbie had plenty of ideas who he might want to work with too. 'We'd tried to put him out with a whole lot of people. You'd know he was going to write with so-and-so at eleven o'clock, and at eleven thirty the phone would ring and he'd say, "I've called a cab." Rob makes his mind up very quickly. That's Rob saying, "I've left already, this isn't for me." He has his

own intuition, and if he doesn't feel like it, he won't hang around.'

The name Guy Chambers rang bells. Guy had been in a band called The Lemon Trees, which had been signed to a label owned by an old Island head who'd been Tim's boss 20 years before.

Tim spoke to Briggs who also knew of Guy. 'I'd worked with Karl Wallinger, a member of World Party, and met Guy at a couple of parties, where we'd had one of those sorts of musician-A&R man conversations that take place in kitchens at parties.' When Tim spoke to Robbie, it just so happened The Lemon Trees had cropped up, and in addition a friend of Jan's had also been talking about The Lemon Trees, saying they were a really great band. So, by a series of coincidences, this unknown bloke Guy Chambers was getting ringing endorsements from all quarters. As Tim and Rob talked about Guy it was almost as though a meeting had been pre-ordained.

Guy and Robbie gelled immediately, and in their first writing session they wrote four songs together, including,

in the first ten minutes, the song that has done more to rescue Robbie Williams' career than any other, 'Angels'.

Another key person who Guy had brought in was Steve Power, now the producer on Robbie's records. Steve, a Liverpudlian like Guy, had known Guy since he was 15, when Guy had copied Steve's pretty much two-fingered keyboard efforts on tour in a band, with multi-fingered work of his own. Steve is now a top record producer with a string of hits to his name ('Space Man' by Babylon Zoo - the fastest selling debut single of all time, 'You're Gorgeous' by Baby Bird, 'When the Going Gets Tough' by Billy Ocean).

Quite a lot of money had been spent making the demos in Miami, and the one song of any worth they brought back was 'Old Before I Die'. In the state it was it was really cheesy, but, in the words of David Enthoven, 'JF allowed us to take the track and completely rework it, which was a huge act of faith, because he had a hit on his hands - but for the wrong group. In that form it wasn't right for Rob.'

Tim has a different recollection about the act of faith:

'Our gut instinct went on the person. As soon as we heard the lyrics there was absolutely no doubt in our minds'

DAVID ENTHOVEN AND TIM CLARK ON DISCOVERING ROBBIE'S TALENT

'The truth is that we didn't tell JF Cecillon. We got Guy to work on it without telling him, but we'd told Briggsy what we were going to do and told him to keep it to himself.'

So Guy and Robbie and Steve Power went ahead and re-recorded it, and as soon as they had a version which Robbie felt comfortable with, Tim and David took it to JF, who to his great credit gave the green light.

It wasn't straightforward convincing Chrysalis of IE's strategy, and Tim and David describe having to fight pretty hard over all sorts of issues to do with Robbie's new direction and image. The artist Chrysalis had signed was Robbie Williams from Take That, and they understandably thought it a million times safer to stick to the 'boy band star goes solo' route.

But the 'two proud dads' felt there was no mileage in that. They'd finish with a 26-year-old failure, or with Robbie ending up like Cliff Richard, and with all due respect to Cliff Richard that was not what Robbie had in mind. Neither did he want to become a Jason Donovan, starring in *Technicolour Dreamcoat*.

Though reluctantly at first, Katie Conroy and her promotional team at Chrysalis accepted IE's strategy, and gave terrific support. Songs like 'South of the Border' with references to Cocaine Katy were just not suitable for nine-year-olds.

There's always the ghost of Andrew Ridgeleys past to come and haunt, so the example to follow was to take the George Michael part of the combo and try to cross Robbie over and make him credible. Now they are on their way to achieving that. It is patently clear that Robbie is not an ex-Boy, and he's not the next George Michael either. He's a rock star with a band in his own right, the first Robbie Williams, a unique act.

The instant chemistry with Robbie was a break for Guy too, a very talented bloke, well respected for his work with The Lemon Trees. As a session musician he'd worked on hits (sometimes with his friend Steve Power, who'd get him in to do bits from time to time when he needed a keyboard player), but he'd never had a hit of his own. He is

around ten years older than Robbie and from an entirely different background. His father is a flautist with the Liverpool Philharmonic, and Guy himself studied composition at the Guildhall School of Music, although he says he spent more time with various rock bands (such as the one where he'd replaced Steve Power) than studying.

'When it was suggested I worked with him I was not sure about it at all. It was in Robbie's heavy period. He was a casualty, and I felt scared for him. He'd had a No.2 hit, "Freedom", which wasn't even his own song, and I began asking myself, "Will I have to do all the work?"'

Like the rest of the team surrounding Robbie, he found a young man full of ideas, and the chemistry between them was instant and strong. Like Robbie, Guy admits to some insecurity, perhaps because his own career had been a bit of a struggle, frustrating for a man of such talent. 'We are very opposite characters, but we are also both a bit insecure - that makes us understand each other,' says Robbie.

After they wrote 'Angels', Guy was ill for a time, with

a migraine. Guy says he is the type that never gets ill, who visits a doctor about once a decade.

'I don't think it was a migraine,' says Robbie, 'I think he made himself ill with excitement. We knew straight away it was a good song. And I think he knew how good it was too, but didn't quite dare believe it.

'When I went to record the demo I got a taxi in the snow to the studio. The driver recognized me and asked what I was up to these days, so I said I was just going to try something out with somebody new. We finished, and by complete chance it was the same taxi driver on the way back. So I gave him the tape of "Angels" and said "Play that."

'He did, and said, "That's No.1 that is…"

'Strange that when the album came out the one song that the good reviews slagged off was "Angels".'

So, there was now close to a Robbie Williams dream team in place: managers David Enthoven and Tim Clark, personal assistant Gabby Chelmicka, Chris Briggs at Chrysalis, Steve Power to produce, along with Guy who

could transform Robbie's music and lyrical ideas into something the public might want to buy. And they had 'Angels' in the can.

The team was shaping up nicely, except that its star player, Robbie Williams, was still a pisshead.

Fortunately, he had extraordinarily tolerant and patient people around him, even when he was incoherent under the mixing desk between vocal takes with a bottle of wine. Somehow they got *Life Thru a Lens*, that crucial first album, made.

The reason for the tolerance and the patience was that they understood what they had. Artists who are both talented and who the public take to are ludicrously hard to find. Too often the music industry either fails to appreciate this fundamental fact - stars don't grow on trees - or they don't care.

At one level, you could say Robbie Williams successfully dropped the super-clean, boy-band image, by getting a drink and drug problem. But at another, it was obvious that this was not part of any kind of strategy; as he'd pop his head up

from beneath the mixing desk and garble something incoherent, they knew they had a sad lad, pretending to be a lad, really because when he was sober he was a sensitive, vulnerable individual.

As Chris Briggs puts it, 'I've seen it repeatedly where talented people are put on schedules from hell, become stars, but get burnt out, and the people who burnt them out go, "Where's the next one?" Well, there aren't any next ones, there's one every five years, and only if you're really alert do you pick one of them up.'

'When hotel rooms get smashed up, there is usually a reason. When artists are found wandering naked down corridors at six in the morning on various cocktails of drugs, there is usually a reason too. It's not just because they wanted to party. Often it's because they've snapped under the strain and are disturbed.'

'From the outside it's easy to see "spoilt, pampered artist throwing wobbler" but I'm hearing alarm bells.' But isn't that what's almost expected of a star?

'There's a difference between a prat acting the rock star, and a talented, sensitive person going into meltdown. To the outsider, or even the tabloid journalist, it may look the same: the archetypal egomaniacal arsehole having his daily tantrum. But there's a difference.'

The story that gets written is the one by Fleet Street's legendary, but apocryphal, girl reporter who'd sit naked at her word processor, running down the pop star she's just interviewed, having snorted all his coke and shagged him senseless.

At this time Robbie, it has to be admitted, was doing his fair share of snorting and shagging, but he was surrounded by people who understood his problems. One time he went AWOL for a while, before reappearing unannounced in something of a state at his mother's. She's not outside the management's support network, but right in it, to the extent that she made her Robert ring up David and Tim and come clean with them about what he'd been up to. They got straight in a car and drove up to Stoke to talk things over.

The cynic who suggests that's because their prize property might have sunk beneath the commercial waves

misunderstands the situation. Yes, they are motivated by money, but they also care for their charge. And at this stage, with litigation between Robbie and his previous three managers still live, and with little to show in terms of product, they weren't earning any. They were all in it together.

Which isn't to say that a crunch point didn't come, at which Tim and David had to say, 'We want to manage you, but you're close to being unmanageable.'

The way to get through to Robbie is not to threaten, but to sit him down and point out that he could be throwing away his huge gift. That line of argument brings him to himself quicker than anything.

The end of 1996 and first half of 1997 were spent making *Life Thru a Lens*. The first single from it was released on April 14th, and was followed by two others before the album itself came out at the end of September.

Meanwhile, Robbie agreed that he should sort himself out and get into rehab, going to Clouds House in Wiltshire

for six weeks in June and July. He was allowed out for one day in the middle for a video shoot, and at the end went straight onto *Top of The Pops* for the release of 'Lazy Days'.

'Last year, when I left rehab, I had to break with all my friends. But when I was taking drugs I didn't have any real mates. What I think of as a mate now is someone you can talk to when you're not pissed. If I can't talk to you unless I'm drunk and you can't talk to me when I'm not drunk, that's not right, is it?'

'It's not that they were leading me astray either. Nobody leads you astray, but people are more than accommodating in helping you with your own self-destruction; no one leads you astray, you do it yourself.'

'I didn't know how to stop drinking. I couldn't do my work, I wanted to be writing songs with Guy, or singing "Angels", and it wasn't going to happen if I looked the way I did and presented myself in the fashion I did.'

On the face of it the album was not a success. It reached a high of No.11, then dipped, seemingly never to reappear. Reviews had been mixed. Some praised the album highly:

'I was blown away... as you are guided through a very personal account of Robbie's life over the past few years from "South of the Border" to the present day with "Clean". A very reflective but positive album...'

'... "Ego a Go Go" is a stormingly addictive whirlwind of funky bass guitar and crashing drums which also appears to be a scathing attack on Gary Barlow. But when Robbie sings the line, "Ego a Go Go, now you've gone solo, living on a memory, where've you been lately, do you still hate me?" it smells of insecurity and paranoia, that only makes Robbie look daft and desperate... a few sloppy ballads too, "Angels" is a sickly sweet symphony, and "One of God's Better People" is a slightly embarrassing acoustic dedication to his mother...'

But another reviewer pointed out that 'Ego a Go Go' could be heard as a self-parody, which was not a stupid comment because Robbie doesn't take himself seriously: 'What I do is not brain surgery,' though no-one denies that,

like many performers, he is fuelled by insecurity, a desire to prove himself, to be loved. So he does want to be taken seriously; but he wants people to have a laugh while taking him seriously.

Student mags were more encouraging, '... I thought I'd take the piss out of this, but found I not only enjoyed the music but played it over and over again...'

The *Yorkshire Evening Post* said 'Oh, dear. Being a former Take That star is bad enough, without sounding like someone trying to impersonate Liam Gallagher on *Stars in Their Eyes*. Robbie sounds sneering, contemptuous, and daft on this forgettable album.'

The *Daily Mirror*'s Matthew Wright picked up on the sneering: 'Industry insiders reckon less than 20,000 copies have been sold. I bet Chrysalis bosses are beginning to wonder what they paid £2m for...'

The *Jewish Chronicle* didn't much like the album, but singled out 'Angels', 'Much on offer here is threadbare indeed, with only the swelling "Angels" offering consolation.'

NME's observations focused in a harsh but fair way on Robbie's insecurities: 'One day he'll be far too confident to bother with bitterness, some day he won't be so self-consciously Robbie Williams about everything...' Though *The Times*, talking about the live show, didn't think the bitterness was such a bad thing, '...maybe he is just a millionaire having fun, but so long as the bitterness is there and the boredom does not set in, this show is worth catching...' So perhaps we should let the cook add the spice and not ask the diners in the restaurant to suggest how much. We should take no notice of those who say it's time he left off Take That. A bit of bitterness is what gives the meal its edge.

Even The *Telegraph* liked the show: 'These songs, co-written with Guy Chambers, are against all expectations rather good... whatever is driving this natural and likeable performer, we were clearly witnessing a man in his element having the time of his life.'

The *Scotsman* reported that, 'There was oestrogen running down the walls of The Barrowlands when Robbie Williams appeared', showing that he still has some way to go to shake off the Take That audience. *NME* said '... in Take That he always had the best voice, the best dancey bits, the best looks and shockingly enough, a personality. Gary Barlow tried to be Britain's Billy Joel [that answer by the way Gary is, 'No thanks you bland tedious schlock merchant'] ... but the Pulitzer prize may be some way off, with dumb-smart lyrics, "her clothes are very rich just because her daddy's rich"...'

Well, as the saying goes, any creative artist can please all of the people some of the time, and some of the people all of the time, but he can't please all of the people all of the time.

In November 1997 his management was sitting looking at an album that had sold only 3,000 in eight weeks, and by December was languishing at No. 104. Actually, languishing is the wrong word. It was disappearing South of the Border fast.

Tim and David weren't too fazed, but the record company was showing signs of panic, wanting to TV advertise in the hope of recouping a bit.

Tim and David's message was, 'No, no, no, what we've got here is a brand new artist. Yes, he was in Take That, this mega huge act, but so effing what, he wants to appeal to a completely different audience. We realized that what we had left was 30,000 Take That fans. We also knew we had "Angels" in the can, and we'd also found out that live shows worked fantastically, so we were confident about what we had as a live performer and entertainer. That was patently clear to us. Our job has been to explain to the record company not to go down the line of least resistance, the route of the ex-Take That Gary Barlow pretty boy image. Rob wanted to be a rock'n'roll star on stage and an entertainer. It's been a battle to convince them, but we've been proven right.'

'The first stage has been to develop credibility in a core market, to get a really committed fan base. Only then can we do crossover things - like film acting - and get

away with it. Until credibility is established with a core market, you run the risk of blowing it with the core market if you try out too much. For Rob to have any chance of longevity, he's got to have that core. Then we can look at a 15 or 20 year career, although whether you can go beyond that these days, like a Frank Sinatra, is difficult to know. With the advent of TV you can be all used up through over-exposure.'

It's been said that Robbie is an actor somehow in the music business, and his father says, 'There's a comic in there trying to get out. When he eventually replaced Chris Evans on *The Big Breakfast* for a week, he used to ring me up and say "Give me some one-liners."' Robbie does want to act eventually, 'but not a cheeky chappie. I do mad really well. I want to do a serial killer, the kind where the outside looks fine, but the eyes tell a different story.'

But with the album at No. 104, and falling fast, the chances of a 15 or 20 year career, let alone one like Robbie's film hero Frank, were not looking good, unless he wanted to end up as a TV presenter. And then they released 'Angels'.

'I can't take myself

seriously because what I do

is very silly. It's not brain

surgery that I'm doing, it's

not brain surgery that

anyone else is doing, it's

just about picking up a

guitar and writing a song

and expressing what you

want to say. It doesn't make

you Einstein.'

The soundtrack
to people's lives

Second album syndrome is the classic record industry problem, the musical equivalent of writer's block. Since the release of 'Angels', *Life Thru a Lens* has become one of the best-selling albums of 1998, with even a chance of becoming *the* best-selling album. How do you top that?

Robbie and Guy were in Jamaica on a songwriting holiday when they heard that the album had gone platinum. Robbie was in danger of a relapse, hitting the champagne in celebration. When another call came in, saying it was likely to go double-platinum (600,000 copies sold), he suddenly woke up to what he could soon be throwing away, as his management constantly remind him, and just stopped.

Lennon and McCartney, McCartney and Lennon, it's wrong to put one before the other. Williams and Chambers, Chambers and Williams. They complement each other perfectly, trust each other completely, but it's far from being possible to say composer and wordsmith, because Robbie has melody ideas aplenty, and Guy's input on Robbie's lyrics is important too.

Seeing them work, which they are happy to do before an audience of anyone hanging around the

house, you begin to understand how creative collaborations work, how one plus one equals three or more. They are not embarrassed at trying ideas out on each other, not afraid of offending each other. They make each other confident, luxuriating in the feeling that, after years of their creative talents lying unnoticed, people are going to like their songs.

'Some tricks just work,' says Guy, 'But we try to go beyond the cliche, not afraid of using them either.'

'We're not scared. With someone else - ' says Robbie ` - I'd feel embarrassed about soppy lines.' The lyrics are mainly Robbie's, but Guy is straight up if something doesn't work:

Fumbling with bra straps

And too pissed to prolapse

from 'Win Some Lose Some'. The word 'prolapse' survived a certain amount of time, before the decision

was made that it would just have to go; too many connotations of private bits falling out of old ladies in the geriatric ward. Not very rock'n'roll (not yet - The Beatles and Stones are still in their fifties).

There aren't many ideas that haven't been turned into a song at some stage of pop history, so 'If you can find two lines which are original, which haven't been done before, it's new,' says Guy.

The new album is crammed with new ideas. 'This album,' says Steve Power, the producer, 'is significantly better than the last. There are a lot of very special tracks. I'm more pleased with it than I thought I'd be, I just didn't think we could go up this much.'

'Not many people are making records that are that good these days. We've made seven or eight songs which, on the radio, will brighten people's days. They will make the soundtrack to people's lives. "Angels" has already done that, it's started to be used at a lot of weddings and funerals, it's become a very important thing in the lives of a lot of people.'

Births, weddings and funerals, 'Hatches, Matches, Despatches,' as Robbie calls them. It's even started to be sung by rugby crowds.

Robbie and Guy have lost their creative insecurity; previously, they'd have dragged in any passing DHL courier dropping off a package, the milkman, or anyone else, and made them sit down and listen. Now they're far more sure of their ideas, and they don't worry about what strangers might think; they know when it works.

'If I'd known that writing songs was that easy, Gary Barlow would have been out of a job a long time ago,' Robbie said in a magazine interview in 1996. Back then he might have been bluffing, but nowadays he's not.

A big influence on *I've Been Expecting You* is the James Bond music of John Barry from *You Only Live Twice*. Both Robbie and Guy are big Barry fans. The album title comes from the sinister Blofeld's catch phrase each time James Bond is captured. Robbie even

has a Siamese cat, a pink-tipped Siamese, white, with pink ears and paws (note for cat pedants; it's a Persian in James Bond).

You hear the Barry music in the song 'Millennium' with a hip-hop beat over the top of it (Robbie's idea), while 'No Regrets' ends with music reminiscent of *The Persuaders* (another Barry theme). Peter Williams: 'The nice thing about Robbie is that he draws from different sorts of music: Sinatra, hip-hop, rap, anything.' Robbie and Guy are big Lennon-McCartney fans too, and the Beatles influence is unashamedly present in their music.

Ideas are bounced around the team of David, Tim, Gabby, Briggsy, Steve, Robbie and Guy. The system has checks. If any of them have a really stupid idea, someone else will pick it up.

There is now a settled (and quite brilliant) band, under the musical direction of Guy, of Chris Sharrock (drums), Gary Nuttall (guitar), Guy (keyboards), Fil Eisler (bass), and Alex Dickson (guitar); all integrated parts of the team. If Guy isn't around and Robbie feels

a song coming on, he'll get one of them to thrash it out with him.

The philosophy is that, as each person has been added to this gang, there is a kind of chemistry. They try to get people who they know are not going to be a pain in the arse, and who they have some kind of pleasant feelings about, without its becoming a clique, closed to outside ideas.

There's a good atmosphere in the band, with none of that bullying culture you can get around some stars: 'You're just a session musician and we can replace you tomorrow...'

Collectively, they've all got that thing of, 'There's no point in making this hard for ourselves, we might as well have a good time, a bit of fun, while being as successful as possible.' They avoid the situations which occur - not just in pop music - where the cost of success is too high.

There is a sensitivity from the fixers in the team, David, Tim and Gabby at IE Music, Steve Power the record producer, which says that to get the best out of

creative people, you take them at their own pace and you don't burn them out. You remain sensitive to how much they can take.

Around Robbie it's understood that if you work with artists and performers you might be able to enhance, but you can't change what's fundamentally there. It's ridiculous to try and impose, whatever you're getting that's interesting from them, it's their own formula, so don't mess with it. You can't do a top down accountant's job on your artist's formula, or insist that while he is in the studio his nose is attached permanently to the grindstone. If your artist has only four hours' worth of creative energy in the tank, that's all you're going to get, no point in trying to get more.

So Robbie wanders off and the rest of the team get on with something else; there are plenty of backing vocals to record, remixes to fiddle with.

Robbie is famous for his short attention span, but people who live off their wits create themselves as they go along. As Chris Briggs says, '"creative" can be

shorthand for " I couldn't be arsed and wanted to watch the football."' Often people who are too lazy to use their intelligence are creative. Often people who don't have a work ethic are creative. But they work within that.

Steve Power: 'Robbie wants to perform, and if you try to pin him down and say "Let's sweat on these two words for a few hours," he goes, "I'm off." He's rock'n'roll, he really is.'

As a child, Robbie was the classroom clown who got no GCSEs, and yet no-one around him thinks anything other than that he is highly intelligent, which, if you meet him, he very obviously is. Steve Power says: 'A short attention span can be interpreted as not being clever, but sometimes it's absolutely the opposite. The boy in class who can't sit still is often the one who's so clever he's thinking, "I can't sit in here all day, I've got to get up and do something." In Robbie's case, it's the magpie mind flitting from thing to thing.'

Of course Guy, who produces the records with Steve, has all these 'I'm an artist' excuses too, and yet is

Strong

My breath smells of a thousand fags
And when I'm drunk I dance like me Dad
I've started to dress a bit like him

In early morning when I wake up
I look like Kiss without the make-up
And that's a good line to take it to the bridge

And you know and you know 'cos my life's a mess
And I'm trying to grow so before I roll down, confess
You think that I'm strong you're wrong, you're wrong
I'll sing my song, my song, my song

My bed's full of takeaways and fantasies of easy lays
The pause button's broke on my video
And is this real 'coz I feel fake
Oprah Winfrey, Rikki Lake
Could teach me things I don't need to know

And you know and you know 'cos my life's a mess
And it's starting to show so before I roll down, confess
You think that I'm strong you're wrong, you're wrong
I'll sing my song, my song, my song

If I did it all again, I'd be a nun
The rain was never cold when I was young
I'm still young we're still young
Life's too short to be afraid
Step inside the sun

And you know and you know 'cos my life's a mess
And it's starting to show so before I roll down,
confess
You think that I'm strong you're wrong, you're wrong
I'll sing my song, my song, my song

And you know and you know 'cos my life's a mess
And I'm trying to grow
You think I'm strong, you're wrong, you're wrong
I'll sing my song, my song, my song

You think that I'm strong, you're wrong, you're wrong
I'll sing my song, my song, my song

Life's too short to be afraid
So take a pill to numb the pain
You don't have to take the blame

Life's too short to be afraid
So take a pill to numb the pain
You don't have to take the blame

able to knuckle down in the studio. The point is that the whole team hangs together brilliantly, emphasizing talent, covering for shortcomings.

As producer, Guy still understands that he needs somebody to organize him, and that that somebody is Steve Power. 'Guy's knowledge is musical, my knowledge is record-making. Guy arranges the ideas, then I'll make it all work as a record. I'll be mixing, he'll be doing final overdubs over the road.'

He is another sounding board for Rob and Guy's ideas, and there are aspects of production that Guy (the artist) hasn't got the patience for; Steve will 'spend three days on a vocal take, making Rob sound like God.' He pauses, then Steve adds, 'Put in the book that he already sounds like God. Anyway, spending three days on a vocal take is too anal for Guy, that's my job.'

Steve is happy to do the really boring bits: 'If you've got a quarter of a million pound budget to make an album, you've got to be careful about where the money's going, about booking studios and musicians.' So Briggsy

gets a ticking off when he talks too much: 'Briggsy, you've just spent five hundred pounds worth of valuable studio time telling me about your horse.'

When recording, they get Robbie to sing the whole song through. 'If you just sing the bit you need a better version of,' explains Steve, 'it can sound flat and monotonous. A song builds to its climax. So if we need a retake of the middle bit, Rob has to start at the beginning of the song, that's the way you get the natural build. What some people do is, they might get somebody to sing all the verses, then drop in all the choruses, but what happens is that it all sounds the same. Also, Rob's a performer, so if you ask him to do one line out of context, it's meaningless to him. You can't manufacture a climax.'

They do a whole bunch of takes, then edit the best bits together. Steve is a perfectionist. 'Tiny mistakes are fine in a live performance, but when it's going to be listened to - like "Angels" was 25,000 times on the radio, you don't want to hear one tiny bit of out-of-tuneness

25,000 times. So, say if I've got four singers singing a chord, I'll go, "We've got to do that again, because the third part, in the third bar on the second beat was out of tune." Guy can hear it too, but he won't pick it up in the way I do; I'm the engineer, he's the musician. I am a check. He can go off on his creative tangent, and I might say "hang on a minute..." I have the experience of knowing how to build a track that will sell.'

'Take "Phoenix", which is a song a bit like "Angels", anthemic. You've got to have an orgasm point in a song like that. In "Angels", that's where Rob comes in to sing the final chorus after the guitar part. Because they've been made to wait for it - you've got a middle eight and you make people wait quite a long time - by the time they hear those final chords people are gagging for it. It gives them an emotional thing which you can't get from anything else other than music.

'It's not trial and error, it's in the songwriting, and maybe people like me and Guy can hear naturally where it's supposed to go, and where the peak is supposed to be.

'Robbie still hasn't had a No.1 as a solo artist, but 'I think we'll have more than one off this album... "Strong" will be a big hit. "You think that I'm strong but you're wrong..." He's not trying to make himself sound cool or special. The emphasis is more "I am like you," almost the opposite of heroes of the past. 'You think I'm strong, but you're wrong ...'

'"Life's too short to be afraid, take a pill..." and why not? The world is a changing place, people used to accept that life got harder, and you got miserable, and now you don't have to accept it. You can just take a pill. It's a very 1990s idea, and he thinks it's right.' (We're talking medicinal, not recreational, here).

'I think the record company might pick up on "Phoenix", because it's got the anthemic thing, it's uplifting. "Millennium" is very memorable. We've had to leave quite a few songs out, not because they weren't good enough, but because we had too many. They'll wait for the third album. Rob's writing is getting better and better, and I think people underestimate his lyrical

contribution. Some of them are very, very inventive. The Beatles weren't necessarily great at lyrics: "She loves you, yeah, yeah, yeah..." The lyrics are the hardest part, they've got to be simple enough to be sung, they can't sound too clumsy, or too nursery rhyme-ish.

'There are very clever lyrics, for example, in "Stalkers Day Off" about a stalker. He got the idea from obsessed fans. He gets quite a lot of letters saying things like, "I am the one, Robbie, who will understand you," so the song is about someone who's come out of jail and says, "I'm back... do you want to see me?"'

I've been hanging around

Just in case you fall in love with me

'It's quite creepy.'

'"Stalkers Day Off" is something that hasn't been done before. It's difficult to find something completely new in pop music, but he's done it with this song. The search for something original could easily sound clumsy, and he's avoided that.

'"No Regrets" is clever too. It's about the break-up of Take That, but equally it could be about the break-up of any relationship and it's full of Robbie's humour.'

You're much too short to carry weight,

Return those videos, they're late

'I think that's Rob making fun of Gary Barlow's idea of being naughty.'

Is the price of being famous to go to bed with beautiful women?

As one friend says, 'The first time I met Rob, we walked from Rak studios to the Café Rouge, and I think he got hit on three times, and it's only 250 yards. I thought: "I'll have to hang out with this bloke more."'

Robbie Williams was engaged to Nicole Appleton from All Saints and that is the end of the subject. 'I've never seen him so mad about a woman as this time,' comments Charlie, friend and flatmate. Not a few of his new songs are about Nicky. Previously his attitude was 'Girls, they're all right' sort of thing.

Having come in 26th as the 'most shaggable man', behind Richard Gere, in a magazine's survey (in a better mag he was No.1) he and Charlie, his friend and flatmate, were going through a list of the top 100 most shaggable women: 'Been there done that.' But then with Robbie Williams you're never quite sure. He likes to say things just to see what the effect will be.

Happy Song, from the new album:
Let's all make babies and salsa through Sainsbury's
'Cos this a happy song
Play on my pink flute butt naked thru Beirut

'Cos this is a happy song

'Ex Take That star linked with...' Whole forests have been cut down for such headlines. He's been 'linked with' some of the most beautiful women in the world. 'You're in your early twenties, and they're interested, so you may as well. I wasn't going to say no, it's all part of the dream. A lot of people stand on the moral high ground and say that's very shallow, and it is, but let me say it again, what I do is not brain surgery.'

Which is a fair defence, m'lud.

A non-exhaustive list of the women he has been 'linked with' includes: Dani Behr; Mel C (Sporty Spice) 'The Spice Girls used to cut Robbie dead at awards ceremonies and the like for ages because Mel got a bit obsessed,' says Charlie; Anna Friel (you can hardly read a profile of Anna Friel without mention of her relationship with Robbie - the press exaggerated it way beyond anything that happened.

In reality they dated each other a couple of times, and went on a short holiday together, as mates do); 'Danish Tasty' Linnea Dietrichson; Denise Van Outen; Samantha Beckinsale; Jennifer Langham; Lisa Walker; Tara Palmer-Tomkinson; Jacquie Hamilton-Smith, now Lady Colwyn (True. He went out with her, or rather stayed in, for about a year); The *News of the World* reports that he nearly married 'Jane' on an impulse; Natalie Imbruglia; a Sexy Lap Dancer ('Later she rang me up. How was I to know the phone was bugged and she was going to sell the story to The *Sun*? At least she told The *Sun* the sex was good. And she didn't say anything about the cocaine.'); a mystery blonde with a seahorse tattoo on her breast.

There was once a picture of him kissing a woman, the wife of a friend, taken from afar. Actually it was in greeting, and the husband was standing next to them, but in the paper he had been cropped out.

Not linked with: 'When in Take That we didn't have much time for women but basically, I did have a girlfriend on and off, but no-one ever found out about her.' Ha!

Robbie Williams often deals with things by admitting them, true or not. 'I've shagged for Great Britain, it's time to settle down...' You can't conduct a gossipy tabloid intrigue if it's not denied, so he doesn't deny things. Ruins The *Sun*'s fun.

But things do get to him: OK! magazine ran an 'I love her to bits' exclusive about his 'love for his All Saints Angel Nic Appleton.' Inside it goes 'Can the romance between pop's brightest couple last? Robbie Williams reveals all in this in-depth interview.' He gets pissed off by this because he'd certainly never give an interview to such a magazine, it's a cut-and-paste job of rehashed quotes and some nice photos bought in to make it look like an exclusive.

He's fiercely protective of his relationship with Nic, and the nearest you are going to get to a quote on the subject is to listen to some of his lyrics, though some you'll have to wait until the third album to hear.

Heaven From Here

No no fear I'll still be here tomorrow
Bend my ear I'm not gonna go away
You I love so why do you shed a tear
No no fear you will see heaven from here

As Chris Briggs puts it, 'Robbie's one year bender became a blend of real incidents and legends. The thing is, he's such an attractive subject.

'There was a picture one morning of Rob coming out of a club. "When did you meet that girl?" I asked.

'"About half an hour before the end of the party."

'"Photographer's girlfriend?"'

'"Shit."'

'The thing about being someone in Rob's situation is that the girl picking you up when you're off your head in a club might be the girlfriend of the paparazzi outside, and she'll steer you towards them for the photograph - and then still try to take you home and shag you afterwards.'

'Not to say that Rob didn't get up to some pretty good stuff, even if some things have been made up. He's had a go on everything; he's been on all the rides in the fair and why not? If he can't get away with it, what hope is there for the rest of us?'

Is Robbie Williams gay?

You can't prove a negative (i.e. Robbie Williams is not gay), but you can prove a positive (i.e. Robbie Williams likes women). Robbie Williams likes women.

He gets asked 'Are you gay?' by every journalist with an exclusive, often as the last question slipped in at the end of an interview, and he's bored by it.

There's no mileage in saying 'I'm not gay.' It would be boorish and homophobic to do so, and also, if you start denying things, immediately everyone starts to think you are what you deny. So he says something along the lines of 'My mind's open. At the moment it's women, not blokes, that get me aroused. Who knows about the future?'

It's said that when he left Take That, the staff at gay magazine *Boyz* wore black for a week. The Take That audience was 95% female, the rest was made up of gay blokes. Robbie is pleased that as a solo artist he's getting the proportion of men in his audience up to the 40% sort of level, '...and many of them are blokes who fancy girls.'

A line in the song 'Old Before I Die': 'Am I straight or gay?' had The *Gay Times* reporting that this 'signals the end of him as a sexually intriguing artist,' though you'd have to be gay to understand why. On the face of it the line is ambiguous enough. The article goes on to ask, 'does he have a studied second-hand sexual ambiguity dropped in because it's supposedly controversial? The real question both Robbie and angry fans should be asking is "does anyone still care?" I know that gay men are supposed to be notoriously loyal consumers, but after these spectacularly hopeless efforts even the old age peds and the G.A.Y. boys must be thinking twice about their respective records in the future.'

Robbie stole the show at a *Mad About the Boy* evening hosted by Ned Sherrin in celebration of the life of Noel Coward, demonstrating that he can camp it up with the best of them. Stealing the show before such a demanding audience is no mean feat, but the audience seemed more hung up on whether Robbie is gay or not than Robbie himself.

Once in a generation

Your author was hand-picked to write this book, selected against intense competition for his complete ignorance of rock'n'roll, and a lifelong love of classical music, but also for his open mind. A good initiation for him, it was felt, would be the Glastonbury Experience, Mud 'n' Roll (there we go, an original pun already). First though there was to be a Bristol University gig as a warm-up for the Glastonbury set.

'Get the tour bus from behind King's Cross at 11:30, Thursday,' Gabby Chelmicka told me. Gabby keeps the boys under control: Tim, David, Guy, the band and Robbie himself. She does everything from organizing his next haircut to co-ordinating his promotional activities.

My first big mistake was to arrive fifteen minutes late. Most unprofessional. But I was the first there by an hour. Very un-rock'n'roll. The driver said, 'musicians are the very worst, always late.' Gabby probably tells them an earlier time of departure on purpose.

From the outside, the coach is an ordinary luxury coach of the kind normally stuffed with American and Japanese tourists, but with darkened windows, to prevent people looking in.

Inside, it stops being an ordinary coach after the first row of conventional seats. There is a small lounge, with four broad, comfortable seats facing diagonally inwards. After that, half a dozen bunks. The bus can be home for the band (after Glastonbury, it's straight to Holland), and it's as luxurious as possible, right down to the lamp fittings. Beyond the bunks, there's a bigger lounge with a long sofa arrangement wrapped round the back of the bus. It's the social area of the bus, where everyone congregates.

The next person to arrive is Andy Franks, the tour manager. He has a 40-something 'been there done that' look to him, not quite as raddled as Eric Clapton. He looks as rock'n'roll as you can get, except that he is obviously very together; it's his job to pull the entire anarchic-looking outfit (sorry, smooth professional machine)

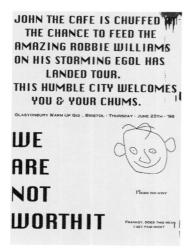

JOHN THE CAFE IS CHUFFED AT
THE CHANCE TO FEED THE
AMAZING ROBBIE WILLIAMS
ON HIS STORMING EGOL HAS
LANDED TOUR.
THIS HUMBLE CITY WELCOMES
YOU & YOUR CHUMS.

GLASTONBURY WARM UP GIG _ BRISTOL · THURSDAY · JUNE 25TH · '98

WE ARE NOT WORTHIT

Please see over

FRANKSY, DOES THIS MEAN I GET PAID NOW?

together. That includes remembering to get the driver to stop the bus outside Robbie's new flat.

Fil Eisler (bass - tall and Czech) and Alex Dickson (guitar - small and Scots) arrive. What is amazing, and refreshing, is their childish joy at going on this luxury pop star bus. There is nothing world-weary or arrogantly bored about them. They are genuinely excited about the Bristol University gig. 'Nice small hall, it'll be a fantastic atmosphere.' They are looking forward to a change from the big venues of the 'Ego has Landed' tour. And they're looking forward to Glastonbury, where, it is hoped, the crowd will merge into the far distance (they're due on at 8pm on the Saturday, a peak slot). But they've got a small boy's disappointment that the bus hasn't got a downstairs lounge like the 'Ego has Landed' tour bus.

Different venues play differently. Robbie felt his show at the Royal Albert Hall had been flat. It was difficult playing to the boxes. Peter Williams was there, and understood the difficulty; 'It's a problem for a comic if there is a dance floor between you and the audience. Gaps

are difficult to play. You need to be near the audience, so I can see the Albert Hall may be difficult to play. But he shouldn't worry. Robert thought the show was flat? It was not flat. If he thinks that was flat, I want to see a show he thinks went well. I was knocked out by it, the atmosphere was fantastic. With Take That there were five of them, but when I went to the Albert Hall they were all there for my lad.'

Robbie had been approached about doing Glastonbury in February. The organizers, perhaps remembering his last big appearance with Oasis, thought they'd like to engineer a bit of a Robbie Williams homecoming. Robbie turned them down. He had no confidence he'd be able to hold a crowd that large – that's if the crowd turned up at all. He was sure they'd all be back in their tents brewing up. His management persuaded him. The non-selling album *Life Thru a Lens* was picking up, and 'Angels' was safely ensconced in the top ten. So finally he relented.

By the time we got to Robbie's house, the rest of the

band was aboard. There was Gary Nuttall, who wears a nice line in pork pie hats, an unassuming kind of guy; if he was pointed out to you in the street you'd never guess he was a rock guitarist. Young university lecturer maybe, a slightly wacky one.

And there's Chris Sharrock ('the best drummer in England' according to Guy Chambers). Chris had been in World Party with Guy.

Guy Chambers himself arrives with his beautiful actress girlfriend Hannah, a recent Cambridge graduate embarking on, she hopes, an acting career like fellow alumnus Emma Thompson.

You expect successful rock'n'roll bands to be surrounded by stunning women, but from that point of view the tour bus is a disappointment: no groupies.

There's Gabby of course, but she's married to Dave Bracey, the band's front-of-house sound man. They have the most good-natured baby imaginable, eight-month-old Ella, with a smile for everyone. A real rock'n'roll baby: when Gabby's organizing something, Ella gets dumped in

the nearest band member's lap; she isn't going to get the chance to become shy.

Then there's Iona Hames, press attaché for Chrysalis records. She's there to accompany a young, male, music magazine journalist who has an exclusive. (These days it's not easy to get an interview with Robbie Williams - the magazines that kicked him when he was down and nearly out in his 'famous for being famous' days don't get a shout.)

As recently as September 1997, a paper reported that Princess Diana's death had obliged a publisher to pulp 10,000 copies of a new directory of the 40,000 most influential people. But it did give the editor the opportunity to replace Robbie as the lead personality in the 'W' slot by Terry Wogan. Robbie, it was explained, was a bit passé... Ha! (Mark Wogan, Terry's son, is a good friend of Robbie's.)

Iona works closely with Robbie's management on who gets interviews. In so far as Robbie Williams is a commercial product, he is protected in the same way as any other product would be, from the Labour Party to Mercedes cars. But as one friend points out, his honesty and openness

are his best qualities. There's not an awful lot of people who could sell a 'kiss 'n' tell' story, because he's so upfront. He's almost unable to keep things to himself, although that's partly from fear of being found out by the press - he'd rather tell them himself. The problem for anyone in the public eye is that it is much easier for a journalist to make an impression by writing knocking copy. To be nice about someone doesn't make much of a story, people want the dirt.

Iona is being bombarded by a teen mag desperate for an interview. She's been sent flowers, and the latest thing to arrive is a chocolate cake from Mezzo. There's no point in sending the cake back, but 'sorry, no interview'.

On this day Robbie has been angered by a piece by Matthew Wright of the *Daily Mirror*, saying Robbie doesn't deserve an industry award for Best New Act, and that he should decline it and give it to All Saints. Bad blood between Robbie and Matthew Wright goes back to Take That days.

Tim Clark once made the mistake of taking Matthew Wright into his confidence. He made it clear that he was

Millennium

We've got stars directing our fate
And we're praying it's not too late
Millennium

Some say that we are players
Some say that we are pawns,
But we've been making money
Since the day that we were born
Got to slow down
'Cos we're low down

Run around in circles
Live a life of solitude
Till we find ourselves a partner
Someone to relate to
Then we'll slow down
Before we fall down

Chorus:
We've got stars directing our fate
And we're praying it's not too late
'Cos we know we're falling from grace
Millennium

Live for liposuction
And detox for your rent
Overdose for Christmas
And give it up for Lent

My friends are all so cynical
They refuse to keep the faith
We all enjoy the madness
'Cos we know we're going to fade away

Come and have a go if you think you're hard enough
Millennium

And when we come we always come too late
I often think that we were born to hate
Get up and see the sarcasm in my eyes

We've got stars directing our fate
And we're praying it's not too late
'Cos we know we're falling from grace
Millennium

talking 'off the record', and told Wright that Robbie now recognized his problems and was going into rehab the very next day. Tim's aim was to ask for a bit of privacy so that Robbie's decision wouldn't be jeopardized. It was explained to Wright that the *Sun* had agreed not to print the story.

Imagine his dismay when the next day, Robbie's decision to go into rehab was Matthew Wright's big scoop.

I'd met the journalist with the exclusive a few days before, at the recording studio, chaperoned by the leggy, blonde, brainy Iona. She controls the press, I've been made to write that. Only joking. He had been offered the most swively, executive-looking chair at the mixing desk, and looked like a little boy allowed a visit to the cockpit of Concorde, pretending he did this every day, but actually in awe. He had that same look on the bus.

When we get on the motorway he gets an hour with Robbie, strictly timed. Robbie tells him how his voice has improved; 'I've never been to a voice coach. I'm still getting my head round the idea that I'm a singer. I should have a

voice coach, but I'm lazy. The first time anyone ever said I could sing was when Tom Jones said at the Brit Awards, "The boy's a great singer."'

Actually Gary Barlow had said it two years earlier.

The Brit Awards were almost a career turning point. 'Angels' had already been released, but at the Awards he won the respect of the industry with his duet with Tom Jones of songs from *The Full Monty*.

'I knew I wasn't going to be able to out-sing Tom, because, you know, it's Tom. My voice sounds like a girl's compared to his.' So, in front of 3,000 hardened music industry insiders, he did his Tom Jones impression. No-one knew what was coming, least of all Tom himself. In the dress rehearsal Robbie gave nothing away, only to arrive at the performance in the complete 1960s, leather, hip-gyrating sex-bomb outfit. By the end they had the whole audience on their feet dancing.

He won over a largely indifferent audience on the *Michael Parkinson Show*. As he arrives in the seat next to the veteran interviewer, he goes, in mock excitement, or

just as likely, genuine excitement, 'Mum, it's Parky.'

When he's asked about Tom Jones, he says, 'Tom, he's lasted hasn't he? It's fantastic, it's like working with an old pro working with Tom...' He pauses, raises an eyebrow and looks at Parky just long enough for Parky to see he's having his leg pulled. It's beautifully timed, understated humour which you can almost miss, and it's very funny. You feel the comic who was trying to escape has got out, but he's a comic not a clown. It's an entirely different skill from the big gestures needed to get a crowd going at Glastonbury, where the raising of an eyebrow is pretty pointless.

While the interview with the journalist is progressing, Iona and Gabby discuss charity requests. Sally gets these by the bucketload at the fan club too. Really it's Gabby's and the management's job. All get looked at, many are requests for an item of clothing, an autograph, something for a charity auction. They try to help where they can, but Robbie has decided it is best not to spread himself too thin; he supports Jeans for Genes at the Great Ormond Street

Hospital, and is about to start helping Ian Dury out with his UNICEF role as a celebrity supporter of the cause.

At Bristol we are released into a dank back staircase behind the University Theatre. Half a dozen girls are waiting, with cameras ready, screaming 'Robbie, Robbie'.

Andy Franks issues the all-important 'All Areas' passes, which allow you to wander into the grandly labelled 'artist's dressing room'. Actually the label is a piece of photocopied A4. This is a student gig. There is a supply of eats, smoked salmon sandwiches and the like, and beer sitting in a big bucket of ice which doesn't get touched.

During the waiting, while the lights and sound system are being tested, for the safety of her young ears Ella is taken to the artist's dressing room. Robbie and Guy work on a song they wrote earlier in the week, called 'Not of This Earth', written for Robbie's fiancée Nicky Appleton. They've also been working on another idea, called 'My Pimp Won't Let me Go'. The 'pimp' in Robbie's case is his addiction. He had been struck by the phrase when watching Jerry Springer, which he finds compulsive viewing, an unfailingly

amazing freak show. 'Why do people let themselves get filmed saying these things?' he asks. You'd think he might know the answer to that.

Later Guy has to go off with the crew to attend to the balance of the sound, so Robbie grabs Alex to supply the chords for yet another song, called 'Uber Queen', about senior gays like Sir Elton John and Sir Ian McKellen. There's the odd jab at Nigel Martin-Smith. The words get scribbled hurriedly down on a scrap of paper.

When he goes down for the sound test he gets Gabby's husband Dave (who sits at the massive console fiddling with knobs and buttons) to lay down a demo tape. There are nearly enough songs for the third album already.

Then we all head off for John's Restaurant, run by a former musician friend of Andy Franks called, er, John. Andy could fix anything, even the menu. There is a delicious range of food, inspired by various Asian cuisines and Robbie's first album. If you are in Bristol it's worth a detour. We are offered 'South of the Border Spicy Mushrooms', 'One of God's Better Thai Fish Cakes', 'Hot

Spicy Fish Thru a Lens' and 'Eastern a Go Go Vegetable Parcels'. At the bottom of the menu it said 'Definitely no pipes or cigars. Sorry. And no fuggin skinnin up.' Well, no one is. Pre-gig the band are even steering off the beers.

Back in the bus some groupies have gathered (male ones unfortunately), Guy's two brothers and another bloke who is telling Robbie what a loyal friend he is.

'I could have sold the story about Nicky for fifteen grand, I could have, but I didn't Robbie...'

He'd have got a few hundred quid tip-off fee. Five hundred tops from the *News of the World*. Half that amount from Matthew Wright. A couple of grand if he'd been able to supply pictures of the couple kissing. It would have been more interesting had he been Robbie's homosexual lover, and had been prepared to sell a 'kiss-and-tell', worth fifty grand at least. But there aren't many stories about Robbie to come out. He's so terrified of being caught he just admits to everything. So you've read it all.

The number of girls waiting for Robbie by the back staircase has swelled to about 30. Our star is beginning to switch into performing mode, and this time pauses briefly for photos.

The support band is The Supernaturals, old friends who backed Robbie on tour. Just near the end of their set, Robbie, Fil and Alex rush on stage. Gig crashing, the Robbie Williams speciality. The crowd go berserk.

After the break the lights dim, dry ice pours out, the lights start playing, and the Star Wars music begins. (Robbie's new flat is stuffed full of Star Wars toys, including a full size Darth Vader suit and a R2D2 telephone. Take That platinums are on the wall in the loo.)

The 'two proud dads' are there in the audience, mingling like private detectives, observing with satisfaction that there are plenty of men, and not just students, there; a heterosexual 30-something fan base. From backstage you get a different view. The front row is still almost exclusively screaming girls. Guy Chambers is having the time of his life on the keyboards nearest the edge of the stage. This is a slight bone of contention; the management felt he was better masterminding the music, rather than cavorting around the stage. Fil and Alex are in their element, while Gary minds his own business under his pork pie hat at the other end of the stage, looking cool.

After the gig the bus has acquired two girls, both pissed and available and very unattractive. Gabby gives whoever invited them on board a bollocking - it's against tour etiquette to invite strangers onto the bus. Robbie decides to go straight back to London after the show. He has to be there for the awards ceremony the next day. A helicopter has been ordered for this purpose, and as it's too late to cancel it, I get on it with Guy and Hannah. Guy, still getting used to the trappings of success, is hugely excited as the helicopter flies at 500 feet under the cloud base all the way back to London, over grand houses with swimming pools and tennis courts.

Saturday morning; arriving at Glastonbury it's rain, rain, rain. Andy Franks, logistical genius that he is, has managed to get the bus to pull up outside a fishing tackle shop, where the entire crew have been equipped with waders and wellies.

Inside the bus there is a strict no-shoes rule to try to keep it civilized. The occupants of some of the tents on the surrounding hillside have attempted to impose similar discipline. Every occupied tent has a pair of muddy legs sticking out of the front door (can't be bothered to take the boots off), with people trying to keep the inside clean. It's a hopeless battle.

There is still some sign that the tents were originally pitched in grassy meadows. But with each footstep new mud is released, and around the sound stages there is enough of it to shame the battlefields of the Somme. It flows down the hill in rivulets, and unless you have a very good groundsheet it must be impossible to stay clean or dry. If you're lucky enough to own wellingtons it is risky to leave them outside your tent - dope dealers have realized that second-hand wellies are temporarily more lucrative. Anyway, no-one has any dry papers.

A minority have come equipped with wellingtons. The rest either accept that they're going to have wet feet, or try to hop from dry patch to dry patch, before giving up and accepting their fate. A lot of people have Sainsbury's bags tied round their ankles. Good try, but hopeless.

We're in E. Coli city. Toilets, even if there are enough of them, are such a trek through hostile swampland that many decide they may as well pee outside their tents. So it's not nice clean rainwater and honest mud coming down those hills and through the tents.

The weather is strange. Torrential downpour followed by shafts of brilliant sunlight, cutting through mountainous white clouds tinged with angry grey, reflecting off the gleaming tents and the mud. The scene acquires an unexpected beauty.

When the sun comes out there's a crowd of nutters rolling in the mud. I suppose it's a case of 'if you can't beat it, roll in it.'

Back in the bus, Chris Sharrock's ten-year-old son is sprawled on the floor. He's bored, there's nothing to do. Normally he would be out there playing football with other kids, or with the band, which has quite a keen five-a-side team.

Robbie arrives from London in the middle of the afternoon with Nicky and Jan. His Range Rover is perfect for the conditions, although it doesn't normally get much of a chance to get muddy. In fact it still looks like a new car, apart from a muddy hand print on the blackened window, put there by a fan who wanted to stare in.

Nicky describes how her mother took her to a muddy rock festival back in Canada. She's quite funny talking about it, and you get the impression she'd have liked to have been out there sliding around in the mud, if the price of fame hadn't forced her to stay in the nice warm bus.

Then, almost imperceptibly the relaxed atmosphere inside the bus begins to change. There's less chat, less banter. Robbie takes Nicky off to a bunk. He needs a hug, it will help him focus on the show. He doesn't look nervous, but there's something different about him, so he must be nervous. Terrified is more like it. This is the biggest gig of his life. The crowd isn't coming to see five members of a boy band. They're coming to see just him, and he's got to entertain them.

Vocal warm-ups for the band start in the back of the bus, led by Guy, arpeggios up and down in different keys. The same exercises as opera singers use; you could forget this was a rock band. By this time Robbie has changed into his stage clothes. There's a quarter of an hour to go, and he has a few interviews to do. He's on duty. He does a television interview; before he answers each question a friend talks into his ear. Robbie comes out with robotic answers, pretending to be a dumb rock star checking with his management what he's allowed to say. It's completely improvised and very funny.

'Stop now, stop now,' he goes, 'Leave me alone, I must go,' and puts a hand up in front of the cameras, before climbing into the Range Rover for the 100-yard drive to the stage. Before you ask, no, he couldn't possibly walk. He'd get his clothes dirty.

Looking down from the stage, a sea of faces stretches into the distance, but the field is not as full as it could be. You can't blame them, it's miserable out there, and it's still a pretty impressive turn out. In the distance people are making their way along a path of World War I duck boards, as if passing from one line of trenches to another, but they're not stopping to see who's about to appear on the main stage.

Then the Star Wars music rings out, and the stage fills with smoke. Almost at that moment a shaft of bright yellow light shines through the clouds, illuminating the whole crowd. The band arrive and 'Let Me Entertain You' starts. The crowd shrieks, then subsides as they realize Robbie hasn't arrived yet. When he does, they all start jumping up and down, and don't stop until the set ends an hour later.

As the set progresses, people passing on the distant duck boards realize something is going on, and begin to turn towards the stage. Robbie shouts to all those still in their tents to come on down. The field begins to fill up.

Just to the side of the stage the 'two proud dads' look happy and, well, proud. They don't watch Robbie performing - they do that all the time anyway. They look at a crowd having the time of its life. Near the front, a couple of girls have gone topless, and are swaying on their boyfriends' shoulders.

There is a ten yard gap between stage and crowd, just enough room to allow the St John's ambulance staff to work. Every so often a collapsed body gets passed across people's heads and handed to the resuscitation crew. You worry that if someone fainted and fell to the ground they would be as likely to drown in the mud as be trampled.

Then quite a nasty fight breaks out, and a boxing ring-size gap opens up in the crowd. Robbie keeps going; maybe he's not seen it, but maybe he's so professional he can play through it. After a while the miscreants melt into the crowd, and a very limp-looking, mud-splattered body is passed to the front. There was nothing in the papers the next day, so he must have been OK.

99.99% of the swelling crowd has missed this excitement and continues to be royally entertained. At one point Robbie gets them singing a chorus of 'Hey Jude'.

At another it's 'Are we going to win on Tuesday?' A huge 'Yes' goes up. (England has a World Cup match). He starts an unaccompanied chorus of 'Three Lions', then it's back to his own music. The 'two proud dads' are positively beaming now, like you've never seen men beam. Robbie's got this crowd eating out of his hand.

The set ends with 'Angels'. It's an emotional moment; the band stops, and the crowd carries on with the chorus. They all know it now, it's entered the public consciousness. Then the band rejoins the song, and Robbie gives it a final go.

Back in the bus he sits quietly with his mother and Nicky. He looks drained, not euphoric, almost in state of shock - and perhaps he is - as if he didn't believe he could do it. Glastonbury was where his troubles had started, now he's conquered it, and with it many of the demons that have haunted him over the last few years.

There will be other demons of course; it's the way this insecure man is driven, but it's also the reason he can be an entertainer who appeals across the generations.

In five years' time he could have been thinking over a cigarette, 'I was famous once. What happened?'

Not much chance of that happening now.

Lyric Credits

'Angels'
Words and Music by Robert Williams and Guy Chambers
© 1997 Reproduced by permission of EMI Virgin Music Ltd,
London WC2H oEA/BMG Music Publishing Ltd

'Happy Song'
Words and Music by Robert Williams © 1998 Reproduced by
permission of EMI Virgin Music Ltd, London WC2H oEA

'Heaven From Here'
Words and Music by Robert Williams and Guy Chambers ©
1998 Reproduced by permission of EMI Virgin Music Ltd,
London WC2H oEA/BMG Music Publishing Ltd

'Hello Sir'
Words and Music by Robert Williams © 1997 Reproduced by
permission of EMI Virgin Music Ltd, London WC2H oEA

'Millennium'
Words and Music by Robert Williams, Guy Chambers, John
Barry and Leslie Bricusse © 1998 Reproduced by permission
of EMI Virgin Music Ltd, London WC2H oEA/BMG Music
Publishing Ltd

'No Regrets'
Words and Music by Robert Williams and Guy Chambers ©
1998 Reproduced by permission of EMI Virgin Music Ltd,
London WC2H oEA/BMG Music Publishing Ltd

'Stalkers Day Off'
Words and Music by Robert Williams, Guy Chambers and F.
Eisler © 1998 Reproduced by permission of EMI Virgin Music
Ltd, London WC2H oEA/BMG Music Publishing Ltd/Copyright
Control

'Strong'
Words and Music by Robert Williams and Guy Chambers ©
1998 Reproduced by permission of EMI Virgin Music Ltd,
London WC2H oEA/BMG Music Publishing Ltd

'Win Some Lose Some'
Words and Music by Robert Williams and Guy Chambers ©
1998 Reproduced by permission of EMI Virgin Music Ltd,
London WC2H oEA/BMG Music Publishing Ltd

Photography Credits

Hamish Brown © Chrysalis Records 1, 2-3, 4, 5, 6, 7, 10, 12, 13, 14,
15, 16, 17 (bottom), 18, 22, 23, 24, 25, 26, 28, 29, 30, 32, 33, 34, 36,
37, 38, 39, 44, 46, 47, 48, 50, 51, 52, 53, 54, 55, 60, 61, 62, 64, 65,
66, 67, 68, 70, 72, 73, 74, 75, 78, 79, 82, 85, 86, 90, 91, 92, 94, 96
© Rankin 8, 19, 20, 35, 47, 69, 76, 80, 81, 83, 95
© Phil Knott 40, 41, 42-3, 45, 56, 57, 71, 77, 87, 93
© Dave Hogan 89
© Jamie Hughes/Top of the Pops Magazine 27, 58, 59

Photographs on pages 9, 11, 17 (top) and 21 courtesy of Jan
Williams
Photographs on pages 31 and 84 by R.S.A. Photography Ltd
courtesy of Robbie Williams

Quote on page 40: Smash Hits, Kate Thornton, 3rd July 1996

First published in 1998 by Virgin Books
an imprint of Virgin Publishing Ltd
Thames Wharf Studios
Rainville Road
London W6 9HT

Copyright © 1998 Robbie Williams
Written with Jim Parton
Copyright in design and layout © Virgin Publishing Ltd

A catalogue record for this book is available from the British Library.

ISBN: 1 85227 743 2

Printed and bound in Italy.

Designed by Slatter-Anderson